CW00868044

EVOLUTION OF A
CHRIST- CENTERED LIFE

EVOLUTION OF A CHRIST- CENTERED LIFE

Calvin Barnes Jr.

Library of Congress Control Number: 2020908437
ISBN: Hardcover   978-1-9845-7853-2
         Softcover   978-1-9845-7852-5
         ebook   978-1-9845-7851-8

Print information available on the last page.

Rev. date: 05/07/2020

To order additional copies of this book, contact:
Xlibris
1-888-795-4274
www.Xlibris.com
Orders@Xlibris.com
812673

Dedication

Marsha C. Barnes,
the love of my life

My legacy:
Jenae
Ja'quaria
Olivia
Ashli
Autumn
Calvin III
Jonathan

Contents

ACKNOWLEDGMENTS

In loving memory of

Johnny E. Owen
Derrell A. Jenkins
Cody Kennedy

Special Acknowledgement:

Pastor David Richardson
Apostle Willie Inman
Merrie Jo Owen
Valerie Johnson
Sobrina Rattler

INTRODUCTION

T HIS BOOK WAS birthed out of my personal evolution of developing a Christ-centered life. If I were to take a poll of my fellow believers who consider themselves followers of Jesus and the following question was proposed, "Are you truly living a Christ-centered life?" I would almost guarantee that the majority of the people surveyed would answer yes. But the truth of the matter is that the modern church, especially here in the West, has no real concept of being totally devoted to Christ. Most Christians live two separate lives: we have our Sunday facades, and we have our secular lives. We try to keep our secular lives for our own benefit, and we keep our so-called spiritual lives for God; and we are all too content on keeping these two worlds separate. In the eyes of God, he doesn't separate our lives by church life and secular life. God sees us as a complete being, and he wants to get his glory through us. In fact, Jesus is concerned about every aspect of my life–from my relationship with him to my career and marriage and every detail of my life. My sincere desire is for you to have a personal encounter with Jesus that evolves into a lifelong love affair, one that changes everything about who you are. I wish I could give you a magic pill or some sort of formula to help you with this transition, but life is a journey of highs and lows. Somewhere within this quest, if you search with all your heart, Jesus our Savior is waiting to become the most significant part of your life. Imagine for a moment the God of the universe standing and knocking on the door of your heart. All you must do is open the door and allow him to come in. Our Heavenly Father wants to fellowship with us constantly; he wants us to go beyond simply giving our lives to him at the point of salvation.

The Bible says in Hebrews 4:16 that we can come boldly before the throne of grace. When I think of the word *boldly*, I realize that it implies confidence. So once I've accepted him as Lord and Savior, I'm now able to enjoy a level of intimacy like no other. The word *evolution* means the gradual development of something, especially from a simple to a more complex form. I caution you to not get confused by the word *evolution* because I believe scripture supports that Jesus finished everything on the cross, and our evolution consists of only discovering through a relationship with him the promises of an abundant life. As you continue to read this book, you will discover the Christ-centered evolution that comes from a life of being committed to the teachings and principles of Jesus. We must realize and understand that Jesus is the source of our evolution. Without him, true change will not happen. I've been guilty of reading blogs and self-help books, trying to transform myself into what I thought was the perfect Christian, only to discover that I fell short. I ended up with feelings of failure and defeat. Although I may have had good intentions and my motives were sincere, I still could not make any real changes in my life without the help of the Holy Spirit. At the time of writing this book, I am two weeks from my forty-sixth birthday, and I have been saved since the age of twenty-two. For most my adult life, I have been in the ministry. The next statement I'm about to say pains me to my heart, but it's a statement of fact and is the real motivation behind this book. For at least 90 percent of my Christian walk (ministry included), I have not lived a Christ-centered life. I was like the average American Christian: I perceived Jesus like a genie in the bottle who was ready to grant me my heart's desire. The Christianity I signed up for was blessings and pie in the sky with no real-life change.

Only after my family was in jeopardy of falling apart did I really begin to discover the awesome experience of a Christ-centered life. Through my pain and tears, I encountered the Jesus I preached and read about for years. Jesus was no longer a figure in history or someone that I knew a few facts about. He was a real presence in my life. I began to long for the personal-prayer time. He became so real to me that my life was changed! The scriptures literally began to jump off the pages, and God was speaking to me so clear. As I began to reflect on my new relationship with the Holy Spirit, I began to develop a burden for Christians who suffered from what I had been through. My hope and desire is that this book will be a lifeline to help you develop a Christ-centered life.

Let the evolution begin . . .

CHAPTER 1

No Other Gods

Thou shalt have no other gods before me.

–Exodus 20:3 KJV

A S CHRISTIANS, WE are very familiar with this scripture, and most of us will never bow down to a graven image, but I am convinced that we build up idols in our daily lives constantly without even thinking about it. God specifically tells us that he is a jealous God (Exod. 34:14). So anything that we hold in higher priority than God is an idol. Whether it's your job, your wife, your home, or your new sports car, if it has your affection more than God, it's a potential idol. If you want to evolve into a Christian who is Christ-centered, you must understand the dangers of idol worship and how easy it is to be consumed with something or someone. Jesus said that we are to love the Lord our God with all our heart and with all our soul and with all our mind (Matt. 22:37). This scripture is so clear and transparent that the only logical conclusion is that Jesus must be first in our lives. Until this fact is true, we cannot live a true Christ-centered life.

Subtle Idols

My idol worship story is not unique, but it's a common occurrence that needs to be revealed so the body of Christ can be set free. I'm married to the most amazing woman on the planet. Her beauty on the outside is only eclipsed by her beauty on the inside. As I look back over our twenty-three-year relationship, I have come to realize that I made her an idol of my affection. I noticed that when our relationship was good, I was excited and motivated about life, but as soon as we were having tough times, I felt that I had nothing to live for and couldn't survive without her. I found myself on an emotional roller coaster trying to make her happy and pulling on her to make me feel secure. The issue I couldn't seem to reconcile is that Jesus told me to love my wife as Christ loved the church (Eph. 5:25). So I rationalized my idol worship by saying, "I am just following your word, God!" I did not understand the errors of my ways until one morning, as I was looking at my nightstand, every picture I had on it was of her! (Now before we go too far, it is *not* a sin to have a picture of your wife on the nightstand, but my nightstand began to look like a shrine.) I looked over at her nightstand, and she didn't have a single picture of me on it! I knew my wife loved me, and I also knew that God put us together, but I had gotten into something that was no longer healthy and pleasing to God. I noticed when she was sad, I would try to do everything I could to make her smile; if she was mad at me, I couldn't function at work or carry on with my daily routine without it being a struggle. I found myself wanting to talk or text her constantly just to have some communication with her. As I begin to see myself, I understood then that the only constant in my life is Christ. In fact, when we try to find our security in anything outside of God, we are setting ourselves up for failure. As much as I know my wife loves me, she is only human and will eventually fail me. If I place all my trust and all my faith in her, I would eventually collapse.

Most of the idols infiltrating the church today are very subtle. We start out generally with very sincere motives, but it grows into a full-blown obsession which consumes every area of life. The young husband who wants to provide for his new bride the finer things in life gets possessed with work and neglects his family. The young lady who's a little overweight becomes overwhelmed with her appearance, and losing weight is constantly on her mind. Idolatry in the church must be exposed so we can be productive for the kingdom of God. Abraham, the father of our faith, was tried by God to see if he loved God more than anything on Earth. Abraham was promised a son named *Isaac*. After waiting and enduring the passage of time, Sarah miraculously gave birth to the son of promise. I'm sure Abraham was filled with excitement and jubilation at the birth of his new son. Although Abraham had a son, Isaac was the one who held a special place in his heart. In Isaac, he got a glimpse of the future, and every day must have been full of joy and anticipation of the covenant God had made with him. Then one day everything changed. The God for whom he left his family to serve required Abraham to do the unthinkable. After decades of believing and crying and finally receiving his son, his God asked him to take his son and sacrifice him on Mount Moriah. How could God ask such a thing! Why would God ask him to give something so close to his heart? The Bible doesn't record the obvious inner turmoil Abraham must have faced, but eventually Abraham mustered up the strength to offer his son to God as a sacrifice. As Abraham prepared to go through with the ultimate sacrifice, God spoke suddenly and said, "I know that thou fearest God, seeing thou hast not withheld thy son, thine only son from me" (Gen. 22:12). At this moment, we see Abraham step into a new place of faith and a new worship for God. Only when you are willing to give up everything for Jesus will he saturate you with his presence, and the Spirit of God is revealed at new levels in your life.

Total Submission

Many Christians desire a closer walk and communion with our God, but very few are willing to lay it all down for the cause of Christ. The evolution of a Christ-centered life consists of total submission. Do you ever wonder why Jesus had only three of his apostles in his inner circle and the others seemed to watch from afar? Our Lord was not showing favoritism. I believe these three—Peter, James, and John—tapped into something that the others missed. Let me give you a natural example. My wife and I have multiple children whom we love very much and would give our lives for in a heartbeat. Each child has their unique personalities and are very different. As a father, I know their strengths and their weaknesses. I understand their work ethics and bad habits that sometimes require my attention. So if I had a task that needed to be completed in a timely manner and it required a real sense of detail, I would call on the child who has proven over time that they can handle the job I have laid before them. My love for all of my children are the same, but I know their character and I know who's not quite ready. Now I believe our Heavenly Father loves us all and that we all are on our way to heaven. However, even though we have accepted Jesus as our Lord and Savior, many of us do not enjoy the benefits of knowing our God on an intimate level because we are consumed with earthly idols that share our hearts. How many husbands would approve of their wives or brides playing the harlot with another man? We obviously wouldn't expect a husband to endure this sort of behavior, but the bride of Christ (the Church) constantly plays the harlot with other gods. Think about this: the Ten Commandments start off with God telling Israel, his chosen people, that they are not to have any other gods (Exod. 20:3). God must become the priority in your life if you want to see this evolution take place. It can't be lip service; it must be in word and deed. Most Christians know the right answers to give, but you must understand that God knows and sees your heart. The Bible tells us in James 4:7, "Submit yourselves therefore to God." Learning to live a life of submission is paramount in our Christian faith. As a disciple of Jesus, I must be prepared to surrender my ambitions, my goals, and my will to the sovereign plan of my God.

Signs of Potential Idols in Your Life

Idol worship is slowly infiltrating our daily lives. However, to develop a Christ-centered life, we must be able to recognize the potential of idol worship. Below are five indicators that will enable you to identify idols in your life.

1. Time consuming.

As humans, one of the most valuable commodities we have is time. Generally, most of us spend our limited time on things we consider valuable or important. God blesses us with twenty-four hours in a day, seven days in a week, and 365 days in a year. If we are honest with ourselves, how much of this time is spent on building and developing a relationship with our God? Most Christians are satisfied to give Jesus two hours on Sunday morning and maybe an hour on a Wednesday night Bible study, but they never go beyond this mediocre state of Christianity. I'm not talking about legalism or forcing you to pray or read the Bible so you can say you met your holy obligation. What God desires is someone who loves him so much that he or she looks forward to spending quality time in his presence and reading his word. When we talk about a relationship, it's something that becomes truly organic. Nothing else on earth compares to this bond of Jesus invading the heart of a man or woman who loves him. The Bible says in Luke 12:34, "For where your treasure is, there will your heart be also." When Christ is your treasure, your time will be devoted to serving him because he has your heart. My time will always follow what I consider a priority in my life.

2. Idols control your emotional well-being. It can make you high, and it can make you low.

Emotional well-being is another sign that something has the potential to be an idol in your life. I must admit that this is one of the indicators that showed me how I had placed something else on the throne of my heart besides my Savior. My personality is that I generally wear my emotions on my sleeve, and it's hard for me to hide how I'm feeling, good or bad. My wife could unravel my emotional compass like no one else, depending again on the status of our relationship to determine if I was living in euphoria or experiencing an emotional crisis. When something can shake your emotional core, you are out of balance. My pastor would always tell me, "When you are controlled by your emotions, you are out of control." God created us to be emotional beings, but we must not allow ourselves to get emotionally entangled with anything on earth to the point that it affects our spiritual life. Our souls consist of the seats of our emotions along with our mind and intellect. Therefore, we must guard our souls from the potential of idol worship.

3. Idols cause you to compromise the principles of God.

One of the most obvious indicators that you may be involved in subtle idolatry is that it has you compromising the principles of God. Jesus said, "If ye love me, keep my commandments" (John 14:15). So if you were once a person who was committed to following the teachings of Christ and now you are justifying and rationalizing your actions, you may be in error. King Solomon, arguably the wisest man to ever live, was caught off guard when he was infiltrated by the idols of the many women he loved. Solomon's life was lived in excess, and once he walked away from the statutes and commandments of God, it was easy for him to fall prey to idol worship. The way to eliminate compromise can be seen in the life of the three Hebrew boys, Shadrach, Meshach, and Abednego. They were ordered to worship the golden statue of the king, and they refused to compromise even at the threat of death. One of the most powerful statements in the Old Testament was when these young men told the king, "If it be so, our God whom we serve is able to deliver from the fiery furnace, and he will deliver us out of thine hand, O king. But if not, be it known unto thee, O king, that we will not serve thy gods, nor worship the golden image which thou hast set up" (Dan. 3:17–18). These young men stood true to their convictions, and God miraculously delivered them out of the furnace of fire. The object lesson is quite simple: we must never compromise the mandates of God, and his word should be supreme in our lives.

4. Idols have a tendency to be the object of your affections.

Colossians 3:2 says that we are to set our affections on things above, not on things on the earth. One of the problems that most Christians struggle with is the feeling of entitlement and attachment. When something is the object of your affection, you want to attach yourself to it constantly, and it gets into an area of addiction that drives everything you do in life. The Bible is clear that we should not love the world or the things that are in the world, and if a man loves the world, the love of the Father is not in him (1 John 2:15). What God is trying to convey to us is that the system of the world is contrary to the principles of God. So if you love and pursue the world's system, you are not pursuing Jesus and the things of the Spirit. There is an old saying that you cannot straddle the fence. When it comes to affection, there is no double allegiance. In the book of Revelation, Jesus warns the church about being lukewarm (3:16). If you want to experience a true evolution of a Christ-centered life, you must set all your affections toward Jesus and the cross. The world will constantly pull on our emotions and human desires, but we must stay close to Jesus to combat the natural man and the lust within.

Generally, when you read or hear about a great figure in the modern church falling away from grace, it's normally due to affection for the world and the system of the flesh. Remember that we must guard ourselves from ourselves. Paul talked about the struggle from within that can overtake the most devoted saint. I believe that we all have a vice of some sort that we generally run to when things are tough. For some, it's food; for another, it's alcohol or drugs. But for the believer, we should only run to God for our refuge. When Christ has your affections, nothing in this world will satisfy you. You will automatically pursue him in your time of need. Think about King David. God calls him a man after God's own heart (Acts 13–22). Amid receiving punishment from God for disobedience, David would cry out, "Please don't take away your holy Spirit from me" (Ps. 51:11). David was not concerned about his kingdom, his wives, nor any earthly possession! He only wanted to ensure that the object of his affection remained, and that object of affection was the Spirit of God.

5.   You participate in the things of God only for others to validate you.

The scribes and the Pharisees enjoyed the accolades of the crowd and the applause of men. They enjoyed the perceived seats of authority and feeling like they were the big shots of the day. Nothing has changed in the church age. We have many believers who need validation from other people. When pleasing someone else becomes a priority in your life, it can easily lead to manipulation and idolatry. As the church, we are designed to edify and strengthen one another, not to make someone else feel intimidated and inferior to us.

Motives are very important when it comes to service of Jesus. Once you commit to a Christ-centered life, Jesus will come in and begin to rearrange your priorities and your motives. He will begin to teach you how to serve in the spirit of love and how not to get caught up on the opinions of men. You must first comprehend that you do not need anyone's validation because you are totally complete in him. Once you recognize this truth in your life, you will be ready to soar and to be the best version of the person God created. In Matthew 6:16, Jesus tells his followers, "Do not be like the hypocrites, of sad countenance: for they disfigure their faces, that they may appear to be fasting. Verily I say unto you, they have their reward." This scripture is pretty much self-explanatory. If we only serve to please others, we are pretty much hypocrites. The only reward you will receive is the temporary applause of men. In churches across the world, we are making other men our gods because our intentions are to have other men pat us on the back. There is only one person in the universe that we should seek true validation from, and that's our Lord and Savior, Jesus Christ. The funny thing about it is that it requires no effort from you because he loved you from the beginning! So just enjoy your relationship in Christ and be who he has made you to be. Jesus, the true model of how we should live, said the following statement: I receive not honor from men (John 5:41).

The great news of the gospel of Jesus Christ is that if we find we have sinned and have built up idols in our lives, we can sincerely repent and move on in peace. We can then spend the rest of our lives serving him and making disciples for his kingdom. The throne of your heart can only have one occupant, and it must be our Savior. Once I committed to giving my heart to God, I discovered that nothing can hold a candle to the presence of the Almighty. When God is truly number one in your life, it's a total shift on how you see and interact with the world. That's when the evolution begins. It begins when you and I begin to see through the eyes of God. Please spend a few moments to take a real inventory of your priorities and ask God to help you align them in a way that pleases him.

The Cycle of Idol Worship

The children of Israel were notorious for living in a cycle of idolatry, from developing the golden calf to going after Baal, only to get in trouble and run back to the true and living God. The average Christian has also adopted this very bad habit of trying to live independently of God, only to realize that we can do absolutely nothing without him. We spoke earlier about God wanting to be involved in every facet of our lives. Anything other than serving the one true God has the potential to becoming something that has dominion over your heart. The cycle is real, and if you think about it, we all know someone who seems to live within this dangerous cycle. One moment they are on fire for the things of God. The next moment, depending on the circumstances of their lives, they have either totally abandoned God or have gradually stopped serving him. Either way they are in complete error of the scriptures. After a period of hard times or just a revelation of how living without Christ is empty, they return to the things of the Spirit. Don't get me wrong; true repentance is always good. If you fall into the grace of God, that's exactly where you need to be. However, when you are caught up in this cycle, you never seem to learn from your past mistakes. You are right back involved in the same thing you vowed you would never be involved in again. Our salvation is not based on works. What I'm talking about is a life change that will ultimately affect your works and will build a life of spiritual stability. Just like Israel, we know what God demands, yet we have the mindset to pursue other interests even if it doesn't line up with God's word.

If I would be completely honest, I lived in this place for years. Only after truly repenting and gravitating toward the Holy Ghost was I able to be free from a life of habitual bondage. Please understand that any sin or behavior that has control over you to the point of you walking away from God is idolatry. The cycle is prevalent in many believers' hearts, and we generally never deal with this issue in our local churches. Therefore, we are so shocked to hear about a brother or sister involved in a major scandal. It seems not to fit their personality as far as we know. Most people are masters at putting on a mask to hide their identity, but the issues of their heart will eventually manifest. If the God of the Bible has not transformed you, then whatever is in you will eventually come to the surface. So if we all have the potential to be involved in the cycle of idolatry, what is the solution? Paul said in the New Testament that when he wanted to do good, evil was always present (Rom. 7:21). A little later in the verse, he continued, "O wretched man that I am! who shall deliver me from the body of this death? I thank God through Jesus Christ our Lord" (Rom. 7:24–25). It's simple: Jesus is the answer. To be released from the body of death, it takes an encounter with Jesus. It takes a man or a woman falling in love with him. Everything else becomes truly secondary in their lives. It's not about making up your mind to do better or to stop participating in a certain sin. It's about meeting and developing a relationship with the God of the Bible. Once you meet Christ, the cycle can start to be broken forever in your life. The most important aspect of this evolution is really knowing your Savior.

There Is Only One True God

In the book of Acts 17: 16–34, Paul is in his second missionary journey, and he is giving one of his signature addresses to an audience at Mars Hill. Paul notices that within the territory, they have numerous altars built to many gods and even one to the unknown God. Paul begins to explain to them that there is one true God, and he is not built by the hands of man. Paul was teaching and expounding on Jesus Christ and his resurrection. I used to read this story with unbelief because I was judgmental. How could they worship so many gods? But my criticism slowly began to turn to conviction when I looked at my own life and realized there were several things I put ahead of my relationship with God. When I began to take an inventory of my time and my personal interest, I was placing my God on the back burner, only to pick him up when it was convenient to my life. The Greeks had a god for everything imaginable, but the truth is that we have divided loyalties ourselves. Remember when I mentioned that most Christians will never bow down and literally worship other gods such as Buddha or Muhammad? We must also watch the other seemingly innocent snares in our lives to keep them in subjection to our God.

God with Us

One of the most important aspects to understand about serving no other gods is to never allow yourself to seek contentment in anything on earth besides Jesus. To walk in the newness of a Christ-centered life, we must recognize that the God of the Bible is ever present with us. One of the greatest messages we received at the birth of Christ is *Emmanuel*, which means "God with us." We need to have an understanding that God is truly with us. He is not some abstract being or a God that we must jump through a bunch of hoops to reach. Once you understand this, you can begin to walk in a new level of fellowship that takes you from being the average Christian to a Christ-centered Christian. The one thing that transformed my mind is finally understanding that God wanted to be in an intimate relationship with me and was interested in spending time with me. In fact, because of the redemptive work on the cross, not only did God send Jesus to die for my sins but he also sent Jesus so that I could stay in constant communion with him and he with me. It's amazing to think that God is jealous for me; in other words, God wants to be the object of my affection. When you begin to understand the relational aspect of your faith, it literally changes your approach on everything. I try not to sin or violate the commandments of God, not because I'm worried about the consequences of my actions but because I love him and I don't want to hurt him. Jesus said, "If ye love me, keep my commandments" (John 14:15). When Jesus died on the cross for our sins, the veil that separated man and God was rent from top to bottom (Matt. 27:51). Now because of Jesus, we have access into the very throne room of God.

Summary of No Other Gods

As we continue to embark on the mission of becoming a Christ-centered Christian, it's very important to remember that the subtle idols that attract us will continue to pull at our spirits, and we must be cognizant of this fact. When you recognize one of the indicators creeping up in your life, recognize it as such, and handle it appropriately. The simple fact that you are reading this book implies that you want something to shift in the evolution of your relationship with God. This shift starts with ensuring that you are not serving any other gods whether directly or indirectly.

CHAPTER 2
Death to Self

Verily, verily, I say unto you, except a corn of wheat fall into the
ground and die, it abideth alone: but if it die, it bringeth forth
much fruit.

—John 12:24 KJV

U NDERSTANDING THE CONCEPT of death to the self is essential to developing a Christ-centered life. In the scripture we just read, Jesus is explaining that if we are to be productive for the kingdom of God, it will require dying. Once I'm prepared to die, I can begin to see major fruit manifest in my life. Only after Jesus our Lord and Savior laid down his life are we allowed the opportunity to enjoy the new covenant. One of the biggest obstacles to the evolution is living in the flesh. Until we allow God, through the Holy Spirit, to kill the works of the flesh, living in the flesh will certainly keep us from experiencing a Christ-centered life. The Bible says that if we walk in the Spirit, we will not fulfill the lust of the flesh (Gal. 5:16). Most Christians are very carnal, and living in the flesh is the norm. Only by tapping into a life of the Spirit can I overcome the power of the flesh. In this chapter, we will discuss the process of dying to self and how it contributes to a life of victory.

The Art of Dying

Dying to self is an art form. We must realize that the flesh and the spirit are enmity to one another. Denying ourselves is to give up our lives to the cause of Christ. Jesus said, "If any man will come after me, let him deny himself, and take up his cross, and follow me" (Matt. 16:24). We must remember that the cross is a place of suffering and death. Jesus is essentially saying that his followers must be prepared to die to everything in this life. Paul made a powerful statement when he said, "What things were gain to me, those I counted loss for Christ" (Phil. 3:7). So what is the object lesson here? Does God want me to be broke and miserable, or is there something else Jesus is trying to convey to us? As Christians, we must understand that we are pilgrims passing through this earth realm. This earth and its possessions are literally temporary. God wants us to possess an eternal viewpoint in our daily lives. We are to live for the things of God's kingdom first, and then we are to concern ourselves afterward with the affairs of the earth. Therefore, Jesus says in Matthew 6:23 that we are to seek his kingdom first. The art of dying is to not allow the things that I face day-to-day affect my spiritual mandate. To be a Christ-centered believer, I must learn to live by the directive of the Holy Ghost. Preparing to die to most Christians is a tough transition. Think about it: depending on when you gave your life to Christ, most of us developed habits, attitudes, and patterns that have been deeply ingrained in our hearts, which sometimes God wants to remove from our lives. Depending on what it is, God must perform some major work to conform us to the image of Christ.

When I first gave my life to Jesus, there were some issues God could deliver me from immediately, but there are a few that I still battle with to this very day. So for me to start living a fruitful and productive life, I had to submit myself to the Spirit of God to cut away ungodly habits that hindered me from growing in God. Once we learn how to surrender our will to what God is saying, we are on our way to the evolution, but this process is painful at times. We are normally at turmoil within ourselves because the humanity in us is fighting to stay alive, but the spirit is trying to reveal God's perfect will and plan to us. Jesus had the same battle in the garden of Gethsemane. He was at war with the human side of himself, but he ultimately defeated the desire of the flesh when he declared, "Not my will but God's will be done" (Luke 22: 39–46). The Bible says he was in such anguish that he had sweat as thick as blood. I believe that sometimes in our Christian circle, we tend to minimize the point of dying to self. Without counting the cost of this process, we might not reach the status of a true follower of Jesus. The word *follower* implies that we are literally allowing someone or something to lead us. Most Western Christians inwardly fight this point, and they put their personal desires ahead of the cross and Jesus's call on their lives. Let's face it: dying hurts! If I was injured in the natural and I was dying, I would be in pain, and the same thing happens in the spirit and soul. So it may be painful to lose certain acquaintances, certain jobs, and even certain things you hold valuable to your heart, but Father God knows best. When the apostles decided to follow Jesus, they left everything to serve the King of kings, and we must be prepared to lay down our lives. My dreams, goals, and ambitions are secondary to what Jesus is declaring over my life. In fact, I no longer belong to myself; I have been bought with a price. In Matthew 16:25, Jesus makes a profound statement that "whosoever will save his life shall lose it: and whosoever will lose his life for my sake shall find it." We must be prepared to renounce ourselves to the point of serving God in order gain life in eternity.

If I obtain a life here on earth and neglect eternity, I'm setting myself up for failure. To build a Christ-centered life requires me to master the art of dying, and then I can experience an abundant life. We are merely clay on God's potter's wheel, and he does with us whatever he wants. Stay on the wheel and remember, God is conforming you into his perfect masterpiece. When something or someone is truly dead, it's no longer influenced by anything on the external. This is the same with you and me. If my feelings get hurt or if I want to fight back in the flesh, I haven't allowed God to kill me in that area. If the devil can still get an emotional rise out of me and cause me to compromise my faith, I still need to go back to the cross on that problem. A prime example is the life of Peter, an apostle of Jesus. He was a man who I believe loved Jesus with everything within himself, but Peter was a loudmouth and had a hot temper! If you remember from Luke's account in the Gospel, when Jesus was arrested by the mob, Peter, the mighty man of God, pulls out the sword and cuts the ear off one of the arresting personnel. So what happened in this exchange? Was Peter not saved? No! It's quite simple: Peter reacted in the flesh in this situation, and he defaulted to natural devices to handle his problem. If you and I aren't careful, we will find ourselves reacting in the natural instead of the spiritual, just like Peter. Let's take another look at Apostle Peter: As time passed, he had been filled with the Holy Ghost and had been transformed into a Christ-centered Christian. When it was time for him to die, he asked to be crucified upside down because he felt he was not worthy to be crucified in the same manner as his Savior. What happened? What was the big change? It's quite simple—Peter finally died to self.

The One You Feed Will Be Dominant

As we continue to explore dying to ourselves, there is a very valuable principle that we must understand. Depending on which one you are feeding, the flesh or the spirit, one will be dominant in your life. There is an old Cherokee legend that speaks to this point perfectly.

Two Wolves

One evening an old Cherokee told his grandson about a battle that goes on inside people.

He began, "My son, the battle is between two wolves inside us all. One is evil. It is anger, envy, jealousy, sorrow, regret, greed, arrogance, self-pity, guilt, resentment, inferiority, lie, falseness, pride, superiority, and ego. The other is good. It is joy, peace, love, hope, serenity, humility, kindness, empathy, generosity, truth, compassion, and faith.

The grandson thought to himself for a minute and then asked his grandfather, "Which wolf wins?"

The old Cherokee simply replied, "The one you feed."

Just like the story of the two wolves, we have two natures battling for dominance in our lives. The one we feed will have the authority in this fight. So if I'm reading the Bible, praying, fasting, and seeking the face of God, my spirit is going to be dominant; but if I am looking at pornography or listening to filthy conversations and I'm visiting inappropriate environments, my flesh will have the upper hand. If I'm walking in arrogance and unforgiveness, I'm feeding the flesh, and I can expect the flesh to attempt to rise in my life. The Bible tells us to mortify or to kill the deeds of the flesh (Rom. 8:13). This war from within has left countless casualties, and if we don't understand the nature of the battle, we can be defeated.

The good news of the gospel is that Jesus has given us power and authority over the flesh, but we must walk in the authority of the blood of Jesus. Earlier we discussed how Paul spoke about the inner battle that we face and how Jesus is the answer to experiencing victory from the power of the flesh. Romans 7:15–25 is a picture of a man struggling with his flesh and trying to find relief from the power that it seems to have over his members. In Romans 7:22–23, Paul says, "For I delight in the law of God after the inward man: but I see another law in my members, warring against the law of my mind, and bringing me into captivity to the law of sin which is in my members." Paul is stating that the inner man delights or takes pleasure in the law of God. But he is fighting the law of his members, which is warring against his mind. He is being held captive to the law of sin, which is in his members. One of the most basic issues is that there is no good thing in our flesh. No matter how you dress it up or what good habits you develop, you are still fallible in the flesh. The Bible says, "All our righteousnesses are as filthy rags" (Isa. 64:6). If I never violated the word of God for the rest of my life, I'm still unclean except for the blood of Jesus. The only way that I'm righteous is if I accept Jesus's redemptive work on the cross.

Now that we have established that our members of the flesh are fighting for dominance, we can begin to starve the flesh by training and feeding our spirit. As we learn to fast and pray, we are literally building up our spiritual muscles, and we are bringing our flesh under subjection to the Spirit of God. The Bible says, "For to be carnally minded is death; but to be spiritually minded is life and peace" (Rom. 8:6). So for us to walk in life and peace instead of in death, we must begin to live spiritually instead of carnally. We must ask God to reveal to us the areas that need to be transformed by his word. The evolution of a Christ-centered life will not be possible until we begin feeding our spirit more than the flesh.

The Importance of Fasting

Fasting, along with prayer, is very important to the life of a Christian who wants to go from a mediocre state to a Christ-centered walk. We will discuss prayer in detail in chapter 4, but for now we will focus on fasting and its crucial role in the evolution of a Christ-centered life. What is *fasting*? *Fasting* is the deliberate withholding of physical gratification (such as food) to help build the spirit part of who we are. As you learn to develop the discipline of fasting, you will begin to sharpen your spiritual senses, and it literally weakens the flesh. Remember the two wolves' analogy: by fasting, you are starving out the flesh and the power it holds over your members. Jesus told his disciples that some issues cannot be removed except for fasting and prayer (Matt. 17:20–21). The combination of fasting and prayer is like igniting dynamite on your situation. Paul said that when he is weak, then he is strong because he is no longer depending on his own ability but on Christ (2 Cor. 12:10). Fasting at the core weakens the flesh and the natural man, and it powers up the spirit and the supernatural man. Jesus himself fasted (Luke 4:12), and he expected his disciples to fast. When he preaches the Sermon on the Mount, he did not say *if* but he strongly mandated *when*, about his followers' fasting. So Christ expected fasting to be an important function of the believer.

We are living in a time that most in the church are not utilizing this powerful technique in their daily lives. In my personal life, when I want to see God move in the miraculous, I default to fasting and prayer, and God always shows up. Notice that I said show up, not give me everything my little heart desires. I understand that God knows what I need and what I can live without.

Fasting flays my flesh and teaches it to obey the commands of the Holy Spirit. Christ learned obedience through the things he suffered. Suffering is the part of Christianity no one wants to discuss because we want the pie-in-the-sky gospel. The truth is that we are made when we suffer for the cross. When Paul was converted in the book of Acts, God told Ananias in reference to Paul, "He is a chosen vessel unto me, to bear my name before the Gentiles, and kings, and the children of Israel: For I will shew him how great things he must suffer for my name's sake" (Acts 9:15–16). God didn't mention Paul's great missionary journeys or that he would write most of the New Testament. What God put an emphasis on was his plan to have Paul suffer. By learning to institute fasting into my relationship with God, I can begin to evolve into a Christian who can recognize the voice of the Holy Ghost. I can walk in a newness of life by keeping my flesh and my members under subjection to the God of the universe.

Humility

Our greatest example of the model servant of God is our Lord and Savior, Jesus Christ. Jesus humbled himself and became obedient unto death (Phil. 2:8). Humility must be a characteristic of a Christ-centered life. If we stop for a second and think about the life of our Savior on earth, we will realize that it was all about walking in humility. Jesus was the King of kings, and he became low to redeem mankind back to the Father (Phil. 2:6). In James 4:6, it says that God resists the proud and gives grace to the humble. God despises the proud, so when we live a life of pride, we are literally separated from God and kept from experiencing his true grace. Pride was behind the rebellion led by Satan, so we must understand that without God, we are nothing. We must learn to become totally dependent on him. The heart of pride says, "I don't need anyone, and I have the power to do it myself." Humility teaches that I must surrender everything to a higher source, and our higher source is Jesus. As you begin to transition to a person who lives and abides in humility, you will be tested on every front. If we be honest with ourselves, we all enjoy a pat on the back or have someone boost our egos, but if we are not careful, this can lead us right into pride.

The Bible warns us continually about pride. Proverbs 16:18 states that pride goes before destruction; a haughty spirit before a fall. This is a somber promise in the Bible that if you live with a haughty spirit, you will face destruction, and ultimately fall in just a matter of time.

King Nebuchadnezzar was king of the neo-Babylonian empire (see Daniel chapter 4). He ruled with absolute authority, but he was full of pride and arrogance, and he attributed his dominion to his own power. God allowed him to lose his mental capacity to the point that he was running in the wild. One day he came to the realization that God is sovereign, and then his mind was restored. Pride is one of the deadliness places to live because we are essentially saying to God that we are in control of our own destinies. In contrast to pride, if we walk in true humility, God shows up as a loving father to provide and help us in our time of need. A Christ-centered life is marked by living in humility to bring glory to God, not to ourselves. And it is is very essential to learning to die to self.

The Defeat of Temptation

One of the biggest concerns that most Christians face is learning to overcome temptation. We are bombarded daily with opportunities to sin, and we are, unfortunately, falling prey to its pull in our lives. The first thing I need to address is that sin is pleasurable. If sin was not pleasurable, you most likely wouldn't be tempted to engage in the activity. But here is the kicker: it's only pleasurable for a season. Afterward you must live and suffer the consequence for violating God's laws, which are pure. The Bible also says that God is not mocked; whatsoever a man sows, that he shall also reap (Gal. 6:7). Temptation is the one thing you must face until the day you die. Now that we have established that we must fight this battle for the remainder of our lives, how do we walk in victory in this area? In Matthew chapter 4, we find Jesus coming out of the wilderness after he fasted forty days and forty nights. The tempter approaches him with a series of temptations, and Jesus gives us the blueprint for defeating the devil when we are tempted.

After each temptation, Jesus says, "It is written." That's our key, my friend. Taking the word of God and speaking it in authority over the temptation is the key. Satan can only present an opportunity; we have the authority to walk away or participate in the sin. As mediator between God and us, Jesus endured temptation. Therefore, he can sympathize with us, and he makes intercessions for us before the throne of God. This is by no means a license to sin but quite the opposite: this allows us to recognize that we are free through the blood of the Lamb. Please don't make the mistake that I've seen a lot of Christians make where they feel that they can fight temptation on their own, only to fail. We must understand that we are absolutely nothing without Christ. We must realize that he alone is our power source. It's equivalent to the television we watch for entertainment. The television has its purpose, and it generally gets all the attention, but if the electricity suddenly stopped working, the beautiful television will not function. That's the same with you and me. Our function is only revealed if we are connected to him. We must realize that God does not tempt us; but if we are tempted, it's because of our own lust that we are enticed (Jas 1:13–14). The temptation itself is not sin, because Jesus was tempted and sinned not. So if we can be tempted and react spiritually, then we have shown maturity in that area. We can also be tempted and participate in the sin, and we have shown immaturity. We just need to repent of the sin. Either way, the burden is on us, as the believer, to yield to the earnest warning of the Holy Spirit in the matters of temptation. As you go through this evolution, you will find the confidence and ability to allow God to remove the power of the lust, and you can live a victorious life from temptation.

Love Not the World

We must understand that we have three major enemies: the devil, which is obvious from scripture; the flesh, which we have been discussing in this chapter; and the world. The world and its systems are contrary to the God we serve. First John 2:15 says, "Love not the world, neither the things that are in the world. If any man loves the world, the love of the Father is not in him." We must note that the world is a system of pleasures and riches, a system that pulls us away from the love of God. Verse 16 says, "For all that is in the world, the lust of the flesh, and the lust of the eyes, and the pride of life, is not of the Father, but is of the world." Let's take a closer look at the following three issues that come with loving the world and its system:

1. *Lust of the flesh.* The temptation to feel physical pleasure from some sinful activity (doing something to make your flesh feel satisfied).
2. *Lust of the eyes.* The eyes are delighted with riches and rich possession, hence covetousness.
3. *Pride of life.* Anything in the world that leads to arrogance, pride in self, presumption, and ostentation.

Obviously, we must live on this planet, but scripture teaches that we are in the world, but not of this world. We shouldn't allow ourselves to be engulfed by the trappings that this world provides. What will it profit a man if he gains this whole world and loses his soul (Mk. 8:36)? In Matthew 4:8, the devil proceeds to show Jesus from a high mountain all the kingdoms of earth. The devil says to Jesus that if he would bow down and worship him, Jesus could have it all. The devil had all legal rights to offer this to our Savior because Adam gave it up in the Garden of Eden. Jesus rebukes the enemy, and the devil removes himself from his presence. Another awesome story that aligns itself with this topic is that of Moses (see Exodus, chapter 2). Moses could have lived in Pharaoh's house as a prince and enjoy the finer things in life, but the call of God was so compelling to him that Moses left it all for the mission God had ordained for him. The object lesson is quite simple: if we are to begin to walk in the newness of life, we can't get enamored by the systems of the world. As you grow in your Christ-centered evolution, Jesus must be at the center of everything you do.

Dying Daily

During this chapter, we discussed the benefits of learning to die to the flesh, but we must understand that this will be a daily process. In 1 Corinthians 15:31 Paul says that he dies daily. You and I must understand that if we are alive, we will have to deal with the flesh. However, as we learn daily to put it under subjection, we will begin to see the fruit of the spirit made manifest in our Christian walk. Jesus also made a reference to us picking up our cross daily and following him (Luke 9:23). We are created with a body, a soul, and a spirit; and we are training ourselves to live by the spirit and not by the flesh. The evolution of a Christ-centered life requires that we pursue our God with everything within us. So what does it mean to die daily or pick up my cross? I believe what the Lord is saying is that we must be prepared to yield to God's will versus our own will every day. We also must not allow the flesh and the pleasures of life to supersede the plans that Christ has ordained for us. God said that the spirit is willing, but the flesh is weak (Matt. 26:41). I've been on this journey with the Lord for two and a half decades, and my flesh tries every day to go rogue. But if we embrace the principles of Jesus, recognize the warning signs, and know our own weakness, we can walk in peace.

Dying daily is not the same as building enough willpower so that you can finally defeat your flesh and behave in a way that you think pleases God. The one message I want to make sure that this book is driving home is that to live a Christ-centered life, it's going to take the grace of God. Think about it like this: if we could have been good enough on our own, God would have never sent his Son to die on the cross for our sins; quite the opposite is true.

We need God to live this Christian life. In 2 Corinthians 12:7, Paul prayed three times about an issue in his flesh. God told Paul that he would have to live with this infirmity, but that his grace would be sufficient for Paul to live through it. To die daily to our flesh requires us moving with the grace of God. I believe a lot of Christians make lofty goals and resolutions, only to be disappointed in their efforts because flesh only begets flesh and the reform we are talking about is spiritual. Only when we allow the inside to be renewed can we see a manifestation on the outside. The scribes and Pharisees put lots of confidence in cleaning the outside, only to neglect the important part, which was the inside, or the spiritual. We, as humans, have a bad habit of looking at the exterior, but God looks upon the heart because out of the heart comes the very issues of life (Prov. 4:23). So the resolution is: a heart changed by the spirit and not just an overhaul of the flesh. Will dying to our flesh daily be a major task? The answer is yes, but with God, all things are possible (Matt. 19:26), and Jesus has overcome the world (John 16:33). We can have days of victory for the rest of our lives! One thing I had to learn in my personal life is that dying to myself required me to surrender my life. For years, I wanted God to fit into my life and bless me with all my desires, but God is the pilot, not the copilot. When you understand that the process of dying to the flesh is propelling us to a closer relationship with Jesus, we will gladly lay down this life for the King of kings and Lord of lords.

CHAPTER 3
Heavy Diet of the Word

Thy word is a lamp unto my feet, and a light unto my path.
−Psalm 119:105 KJV

R EMEMBER THE STORY of the two wolves in chapter 2: in the analogy, the wolf that you feed is going to win the fight for dominance in your life. As Christians, a heavy diet of God's word is mandatory. I believe the church is suffering from spiritual malnutrition because of the lack of reading and studying the Bible. There are two major diet deficiencies in the church, and both are as equally lethal to your spiritual well-being. The first we touched on a little. It's when the believer is getting little to no word at all. Jesus said in Matthew 4:4 that man does not live by bread alone, but by every word that proceeds out of the mouth of God. We must realize that God's word is going to give us strength and help us in the time of need. The word teaches and trains us in the ways of God. As we read the Bible, it begins to convict us of sins, and it also provides us with comfort and peace. The Logos, or written word, is what sustains us as believers. If you are not digging into it daily, you are living a deficient spiritual life. Just like my natural body needs food for it to run at its optimum, it's the same thing with the word in the life of a Christian.

The second lethal problem affecting the church is what I call the "sugar gospel." This is the message of fluff that generally has no substance behind it. Remember the old saying "You are what you eat"? That's the message I received growing up in the 1980s as a kid. Basically, they were saying to us that if we consumed healthy foods, we could expect healthy results, and if we developed a diet of junk food, we could expect the perils of an unhealthy life. The same message translates to reading the Bible and allowing it to take residence in your heart. Picture this: if I only feed my natural body cookies and candies and a diet of sweets, I would be lacking the vitamins and nutrients my body needs to function properly. That's what we are experiencing in a lot of the lives of Christians. We only want the word that makes us feel good, not the word that comes to convict and challenge us to have a true-life change. The truth of God's word is paramount to our Christian walk; without it, we are like a ship without a sail—with no direction at all. The Bible says, "Thy word is a lamp unto my feet and a light unto my path" (Ps. 119:105). This speaks of light that illuminates our paths. When I think about light, I ponder on how it allows us to see and helps our vision in the darkness. It's the word of God that represents a lamp and a light in the scripture. No word, no light; much word, much light. So as we begin to grow in our evolution of the Christ-centered life, the discipline of personal Bible study will be essential.

Hearers and Doers of the Word

In Matthew 7:24–27, Jesus gives a story about two builders: one he called wise and the other he called foolish. The scripture reads as follows:

> Therefore, whosoever heareth these saying of mine, and doeth them, I will liken him unto a wise man, which built his house upon a rock: And the rain descended, and the floods came, and the winds blew, and beat upon that house; and it fell not: for it was founded upon a rock. And every one that heareth these sayings of mine, and doeth them not, shall be likened unto a foolish man, which built his house upon the sand: And the rain descended, and the flood came, and the winds blew, and beat upon that house; and it fell: and great was the fall of it.

Jesus was teaching us a profound lesson: If we hear his word and apply it to our lives, we will be setting up our lives on a solid foundation. However, if we do the opposite, we would be building on a shaky foundation that would eventually collapse. As Christians, our foundation must be secured and anchored in the word of God. When a builder is constructing a new house, the foundation is the most important aspect of the home. If the foundation is weak, then the entire structure is weak. If you build and develop a strong foundation, then the rest of the house is secure and strong. In this Christian walk, we must allow the word to form a solid foundation so we can be productive for the kingdom of God.

For years, I admit that I was like the average Christian. I would read my word at church, but I read it very little in my private time. Now that I look back and reflect on those times, I was very shallow and carnal, and I lived by my emotions. I would explode at the drop of a dime! Keep in mind that I was saved and on my way to heaven, but I was not effective for the kingdom of God because my life couldn't be an example for Christ. I lacked the word in my heart. The word must be a part of who you are as a believer. David said, "Thy word have I hid in my heart, that I might not sin against thee" (Ps. 119:11). What David was referring to was that if the word has changed his heart, then his actions would follow.

In three of the Gospels, or the synoptic Gospels, Jesus taught about the parable of the sower (Matt. 13:1–23; Mark 4:1–20; Luke 8:1–15). A sower sows seed. Some seeds fall on the wayside, some on rocky ground, some among the thorns, and some on good ground. Only when the seeds land on the good ground do they produce much fruit. Jesus gives us the understanding of this parable in detail. When someone hears the word of God and does not understand it nor applies it, the evil one comes and snatches away what has been sown in his heart. This is the wayside. The rocky ground is when someone hears and receives the word with joy, only to discover that the word has no root, but endures for a while. When tribulation or persecution comes for the sake of the word, he falls away. When the seed is fallen among the thorns, the cares of this world and the deceitfulness of riches choke out the word that was sown in the individual's life. Only when the seed of the word falls on good ground does a person comprehend and understand, and he can bring forth much fruit. The Bible says there can be a thirty-, sixty-, or hundredfold increase. So we must ask the question: how many people are hearing God's word and bringing forth much fruit? In most churches, we are counting the minutes on our watches when we can leave!

This evolution can only take place when the word has become a serious priority in our lives. Our adversary, the devil, will fight us constantly to keep us from hearing the teachings of the Bible. We must recognize his tactics and pursue the word of God like it is gold. As we grow in our understanding of the Bible, we begin to set ourselves apart from the average believer, and our walk with the God of the universe will take on a new life of its own. No longer will reading the Bible be a dull routine, but you will discover that God is speaking volumes into your spirit. Every day can be a new adventure in the quest of knowing him more intimately. Learning to hear the word and apply it to your life should take you to a place of growth that elevates the level of revelation in your life. To get to the deep things of God requires a discipline of studying his word. Just like in the natural, I can set an entire table of food in front of you, but it's still your responsibility to partake the food on the table to get what you need. As we continue to allow God to change us from the inside out, no transformation can take place without the word of God. Just like a person working out in the gym, if you want to get positive results, you must be willing to put in the effort; and it's the same thing with reading God's word. The person that commits to a life of studying his word can experience the evolution of a lifetime and walk in victory in every area of life.

Encouragement and Conviction

The word of God is a source of encouragement and a source of conviction. As Christians, we must understand that conviction by the Holy Spirit is a good thing. When God is convicting us of wrongdoing, he is showing us love because he desires that we grow beyond temptation and sin. Only when we embrace the word can we see the fruit of the spirit manifest in our lives. Have you ever noticed that Bible study and Sunday school generally has the least attendance of any service in church? To develop the Christ-centered life, we must commit to a healthy dose of revelation that comes from the Bible. As we begin to read and study, we will begin to see God reveal himself to us like never before. Most Christians are satisfied with the status quo, but if you are hungry and thirsty for the deep things of God, you start by adopting his word into your everyday life. I remember watching people of faith worship and talk about God like he was a real person. I wondered for years about what was missing in my relationship with God. I want what the mature saints were talking about! My desire to know him began to consume my life. I longed to know him, and I became excited about his word. No longer was I content to only know facts about my Savior. I needed the word to become alive in my life.

Knowing Him through the Word

Think about it in these terms: I can give you a few facts about Michael Jordan, and they would be completely true. I could tell you which college he attended. I can mention the numerous championships he's won. I can even tell you how many basketball MVPs he has taken home. But if you asked Michael Jordan if he knew me, his answer would be no! Even though I knew true facts about him, I don't have a relationship with him. Many people are doing this very thing in the church. We know facts about Jesus, but we have no real relationship with him. The Bible says that the children of Israel knew God's acts, but Moses knew his ways (Ps. 103:7), and if you want to be a Christian who knows the ways of our Savior, you should read the word of the living God. This evolution is about knowing this God who gave his only Son to die for us. When you understand that his word is pointing you to him, you will develop a renewed sense of urgency in your spiritual walk. It's not about obtaining head knowledge, but it's an issue of the word transforming you into the image of Christ. The word should be the bar that we measure our lives against. We aren't trying to be good to be saved, but we are following his word because we are saved.

There are many believers who visit churches all over the world, who hear the word, who never go to the next step of application, and who end up leading defeated lives. Let's commit to hearing what the Spirit is saying to the church and being what God has called us to be. Only when we put his word into practice will we see the evolution of a Christ-centered life manifested. As you commit to reading the Bible, you will learn and understand the attributes of God. You will get a sense of what pleases him, and you will find yourself changing into a Christian who can make a real difference in the world. I believe the reason the enemy fights us so much on reading the word is that once we get a picture of God's will for our lives, everything changes. We become a mighty weapon for the kingdom of God. Imagine if we change our approach about the word: I'm reading to know you, God, and not just to gain head knowledge. It's a paradigm shift that bleeds over to every facet of our lives. The Bible must be the final authority in the life of the believer. When you understand that all scripture is given by the inspiration of God, you will begin to realize that it is not an ordinary book of instructions. We are living in a day that everyone wants a prophetic word. I do agree that prophecy is important in the function of the church, but even prophecy must line up with scripture. If you receive a word from anyone that's contrary to the Holy Scriptures, don't receive it as from God! He will never speak outside the confines of his written word. I must admit that there was a time in my spiritual walk when I was in constant search for a juicy word of prophecy. I found out quickly that everyone did not always prophesy the sovereign will of God, and many times I experienced men and women of God giving me words that went contrary to what God was saying in my life. Many of today's Christians are lazy when it comes to the word. We would rather get a word of prophecy instead of reading and seeking God for ourselves. The evolution of a Christ-centered life will only be revealed once the word is a matter of vital importance to your spiritual walk. As we explore and navigate the teachings of Jesus, the flesh will become subject to the word that's in your heart.

The power of following the commandments outlined in the Bible will change the direction of your life. By following his word, I've seen countless number of people make a complete 180-degree turn in their lives. The power of Christ has transformed them into Christians who represent Jesus in their everyday lives. If you want to see this happen in your life, commit to reading his word. The Bible refers to us as Christians (people who are to be Christlike), so to discover Jesus's character, we must get a heavy diet of God's word. If you can muster up the spiritual fortitude to apply yourself to studying and learning the scriptures, the return is remarkable. I wish I could pray for you to receive insight and revelation, but this can only be received by the Holy Ghost and seeking him out in the Holy Scriptures. At the cross, Jesus said, "It's finished" (John 19:30). He has given us access to the Father by the redemptive work of the cross. Now you can build a lifelong relationship with the King of kings. Once you are willing to seek him out like the most valuable treasure on earth, then you will find him. My prayer is that as you read this book, you comprehend that the word is no longer just a book to be read in church, but it's our God reaching from heaven to speak to us about everything that concerns you and me.

CHAPTER 4

Pray without Ceasing

Pray without ceasing.

–1 Thessalonians 5:17 KJV

PRAYER IS ANOTHER important aspect of developing a Christ-centered life. We generally learn about prayer as very small children, but unfortunately, many Christians rarely go beyond the childhood interpretation of prayer. In this chapter, we will answer two questions: Why should we pray? And what's the importance of prayer? Many believers see God as a make-believe guy-in-the-sky whom we can ask for what we need in our lives, and we never grow to the stature of what Christ intended prayer to be. Prayer's basic definition at its simplest form is communication with our Heavenly Father. Jesus, our perfect model, was a person of constant prayer and communication with the Father. All humans have the opportunity to be able to access a Holy God, through Jesus's death, burial, and resurrection. Most Christians, unfortunately, never take advantage of the fact that we can come boldly before his throne and that our God is desiring to communicate with us all the time. Communication is very important to building any relationship. When I met my wife, we initially lived in two different states, but we both spent lots of time and money so that we could stay in touch and build our relationship. This holds true also in our

Christian walk. The more time you spend in prayer and communicating with God, the more in-depth the relationship becomes. One of the biggest mistakes most Christians make is that we settle for just being saved. Don't get me wrong—salvation is the most important issue when it comes to our live as Christians, but fellowship takes our salvation to another level.

We all have relatives whom we love, and we, unfortunately, don't have a great level of fellowship with them. But just because you don't have great fellowship with them doesn't mean that you are not related. Many Christians have been born again and are on their way to heaven, but they don't enjoy the benefits of fellowshipping with the Holy Ghost because they choose not to make prayer a priority in their lives. Or, on the other hand, they only pray when they want something from God. Imagine a husband and wife who had been married for fifteen years, but the only time they communicated was when the wife wanted something from the husband, or the husband wanted something from the wife. We would all be appalled and would label both the husband and wife as selfish and a user. Now translate the same mentality into our spiritual walk. Picture the God of the universe who sent his only Son to die for our sins so we could have an intimate relationship with him. Then we have the audacity to only seek him when we want our carnal needs met! Our prayer life must go beyond asking that our needs be addressed. We must learn to seek God just to know who he is. The children of Israel had an opportunity to talk with God, and they defaulted to Moses instead of understanding the privilege of person-to-person communication (Exod. 20:19). True intimacy is developed when there's only a few involved. People enjoy praying when there are big crowds in which they can impress others, but real growth comes from being alone with God. The evolution of a Christ-centered life will not exist until we pray for God's will to be accomplished in our life. As you read this book, I hope the theme is coming clear that we are to seek God to live a truly Christ-centered life.

The Frequency of Prayer

I remember growing up with the old AM/FM radios and the importance of signal strength on the radio. When you had a clear signal, you could hear the radio and enjoy the music being projected from the station, but if you ever found yourself in-between stations or not getting a strong signal, you had a hard time hearing the station clear. Jesus said in John 10:27, "My sheep hear my voice, and I know them, and they follow me." We are living in a time in the modern church when many believers have a hard time hearing the voice of God. To know the distinct voice of God requires spending time in prayer. Once you get accustomed to hearing his voice, the frequency becomes clearer. My wife of twenty years can call me on the phone, and before she says anything about identifying herself, I know it's her because I recognize her voice. The same thing will hold true with our Heavenly Father: the more time you spend in prayer and communication with the Holy Ghost, the more acquainted you will become to his voice in your life. Christianity is more than a religion; it should be a relationship that affects everything about who we are as people. When I began to change my approach about prayer, I no longer became bored and preoccupied. I began to look forward to spending time with Jesus. I remember loving to have the house to myself because I could be alone with the Holy Spirit. My daily commutes began to take on a whole new light because of the private time I spent with God.

Keep in mind that the devil tries everything in the world to interfere with the frequency of the Holy Ghost. He sets up distractions and turmoil in our lives to keep us from picking up on what the Spirit is saying to us. I grew up in the Pentecostal Church. The old-time Christians would always talk about having Jesus on the main line. They were referring to the fact that you could access God at any time in your life, and when you begin to hear the Holy Ghost speak, you are ready to begin to see a new level of revelation in your walk. Speaking of signal strength, my cell phone is reliable, but there are times that if I'm in a dead area that my reception is not as good. We as Christians must be careful that we don't stay in dead areas too long that will break communication with the Spirit of God. Jesus said he will never leave us nor forsake us (Heb. 13:5). So God never leaves us, but we have a tendency of getting off course that can affect the fellowship he wants with us. The key to understanding God's heart with prayer is to picture a relationship with a loved one that you enjoy. You long to talk and communicate with this individual. This is our God's desire in prayer. He wants to be with us constantly; he adores us as the apple of his eye, and if we can ever grasp this fact, our prayer life will never be the same again.

Staying in the Closet

As Christians, we must understand one important key to our prayer life: God loves an individual who stays in his or her private prayer closet. A prayer closet can be anywhere that allows you time and space to be with God alone without any interruptions. When I want to be intimate with my spouse, I don't want anyone else around. Believe it or not, when God wants to be real intimate with you and me, he wants us all to himself. One thing I have learned with my personal walk with Jesus is that he knows every mistake and sin we have committed, yet he still chooses to love and forgive us. Most people express love with conditions attached and generally have ulterior motives, but God is so different that he embraces us even when we don't deserve it. So if God, being different from everyone else, chooses to love us despite our sins, we should be willing to devote private time in his presence. When you become comfortable with being alone with our Savior, that's when your prayer life takes on new meaning. Moses was alone when God spoke to him from the burning bush. Jesus got away quite a bit to spend time with God. The prayer closet teaches you how to hear God and how to develop a sense for what pleases our Savior. Only when you learn to be alone in your prayer closet can you really experience a Christ-centered life.

The evolution of the Christ-centered life is learning that Jesus is truly our center, and everything else is secondary to that fact. Most Christians are not living this way, so to reach the deeper depths of our faith, you must be willing to go at it alone. If you want to be used mightily by God, stay in your prayer closet. If you want true revelation from the Spirit, stay in your closet. If you want to change the world for Jesus, show him you are willing to pray when no one else has the desire, and he will reward you openly. It's truly all about your private time in his presence. My preaching changed once I understood this fact, and my understanding of God's word transformed me once I got a grasp of this principle in my life. In the spirit realm, if you have been privately seeking the things of the spirit, it will ultimately manifest into the public eye. Commit today to spending quality time with our Savior, and you can see the evolution take place in your life.

The Lord's Prayer (Jesus's Example of How We Should Pray)

In Matthew 6: 9–13, Jesus gives his disciples a great road map to prayer. Although Jesus gave this example, we are not required to pray this verbatim. We must understand that the Lord's Prayer consists of a short introduction, or preface, and then it contains seven petitions. I believe there is an important object lesson that Jesus is trying to teach us in this prayer model.

Our Father. We are to realize that God is our Heavenly Father, so we can approach him boldly and depend on him like a child. Like any good father, God has our best interest in mind.

Who art in heaven. This puts a distinction on our Heavenly Father. There is no other father in heaven. We are making a connection to the things in the spirit realm, not the earthly realm. We must realize that we are aliens passing through this earth. We are spiritual people that live in a body, and we can access our Heavenly Father in heaven at any time.

Hallowed be thy name. This tells us that we should revere and honor his name above all on earth.

Thy kingdom come. Very powerful statement. Jesus is letting us know that his kingdom is not of this earth, so we need to operate in the parameters of his kingdom. We are believing that his kingdom will be more powerful than the earthly realm.

Thy will be done on earth as it is in heaven. After we have prayed that his kingdom come, we desire that his will be manifested on earth to align with what heaven has declared. Heaven has a plan, and we must be willing to submit to the sovereign will of God. As we submit to the will of God's plan, we can see his glory truly manifested.

Give us this day our daily bread. At this point, we can ask for natural things, as well as things to satisfy our spiritual self daily. God wants us to depend on him for our survival, whether it's food, clothing, or anything else we consider significant in our lives.

Forgive us our trespasses as we forgive them that trespass against us. Repentance is such a powerful principle of Christianity. It's literally telling God that you understand that you hurt him, you have changed your heart and mind, and you will never participate in that activity again. Yes, we do make the same mistakes again, but in your heart, you have committed to move on and trust that his grace will help you overcome. We also must be willing to forgive others who sin against us so that we can enjoy forgiveness from our Heavenly Father.

Lead us not into temptation. We must believe that God helps us to escape all temptations and the dangers of sin. When we are tempted, it's not by God, but our flesh is tempted. God knows we will be tempted, and he provides a way of escape; but we must also understand that the temptation itself is not sin. Only when you indulge in it that it constitutes sin, and sin leads to death.

But deliver us from evil. We are asking God to dispatch his angels around us for protection and to help us stay mindful that evil is present. As we learn to pray, we can access God's divine protection for every area of our lives.

Amen. This is agreement with the prayer, and we know that God hears us if we pray in the name of Jesus.

So as we begin to seek God in our prayer life, we will grasp hold of the Lord's Prayer and the importance of what Christ showed the disciples. We can begin to see powerful results happen as evidence that we are praying correctly.

Going to God as Judge

In the book *Navigating the Courts of Heaven*, written by Robert Henderson, the author goes into detail about approaching God as judge. In Luke 18:1–8, we find an unjust judge convening over the court where a widow woman is trying to have a verdict rendered in her favor. The Bible teaches us that this judge did not fear God or man, but because this woman was very persistent in her request, he granted her the verdict she sought after. Jesus was not commending the unjust judge, but he was showing how if we are persistent in prayer that our God would honor our request. But there is something else hidden in this story, and we must get an understanding of the meaning.

This lady was going to the judge who held jurisdiction over her case to get a godly verdict rendered. Once she got her legal affairs in order, the matter was finished. The same is true for you and me: if we go to God as the Judge of the universe and get him to make a declaration over our lives, everything in heaven and earth must submit to what God has declared. If we can gain a legal, binding order from God, we can begin to enjoy victory in our lives. It's not us declaring out of our emotions and shouting all kinds of scripture, but it's about God setting a legal precedence in our lives. It's God who speaks things into existence and not us. We only learn to speak what God has legally said we can speak. Once we have a legal, binding verdict from the throne room of God, everything must shift. In Mathew 18:18, Jesus tells us, "Whatsoever ye shall bind on earth shall be bound in heaven: and whatsoever ye shall loose on earth shall be loosed in heaven." This famous scripture is a legal concept that tries to teach us about the authority we have when legal matters have been decreed by the Judge of heaven.

Once I understand what God has said in the heavenly court, now I can walk in the new authority I have in God's kingdom. The widow's persistence paid off because she had the foresight to go to the judge that could make a difference in her situation. You and I must know that God's verdicts are supreme on earth. Just like our legal system is enforced by natural judges, so is the kingdom of God enforced by the Judge of the universe. Jesus is our mediator, or in other words, he is our legal advocate, presiding in the courts of heaven on our behalf. When God bangs the gavel in our favor, the entire universe must honor what he has decreed. Our prayer must elevate to the place that we, at times, must approach our Heavenly Father in the capacity of a Judge of all.

The evolution of a Christ-centered life cannot exist until our prayer life goes beyond the normal patty-cake prayers that we are accustomed to. As a Christian, prayer is like oxygen to the human body. We all agree, and science supports that without oxygen, our bodies cannot live for long. Once enough time has passed without an adequate supply of oxygen, our natural bodies will die. I believe there is a major epidemic of Christians who have a very weak prayer life, and they are dying spiritually and living very ineffective lives. Praying without ceasing must be a constant mandate in the life of a Christian. Once you discover this powerful principle, you can begin to soar beyond the eagles and embrace the concept of this evolution. In closing, remember that everyone we admire in the Bible and hold in high regard only got to that place by praying and spending time with God. If you are to make a sincere difference on the planet, prayer must be a discipline that you practice.

CHAPTER 5

Understanding Your Identity

*Therefore, if any man be in Christ, he is a new creature: old
things are passed away; behold, all things are become new.*

—2 Corinthians 5:17 KJV

O NE OF THE most important aspects
of Christianity is understanding who
you are in Christ. As believers, we must understand that God has a unique plan
and purpose for our existence. We must understand that God has placed in each
of us a legacy that he wants us to leave out on the earth. For years I walked
around with an identity crisis and feeling inferior to anyone whom I perceived
to have a level of success. I came out of a sales background that thrives on
competition, and if I'm honest, I had the same experiences in the church. I've
experienced everything, from preachers wanting to prove that they can excite
the crowd more than another preacher to choir members arguing about who's
going to lead the pastor's favorite song. The competition in the church isn't
broadcasted. It's very subtle, and it's a poison that will continue to contaminate
our churches until we get a grasp of who we are in Christ. The Bible teaches
that we are one body with many members (1 Cor. 12:12). Paul is teaching us
that everyone has a mission and a purpose to fulfill in the body of Christ. As
I reflect on the years I spent not understanding my place in God's kingdom, I

realized that it was equivalent to wearing a mask. People generally wear masks to hide their identity, and I hid it well. The problem with wearing a mask is that it eventually falls off, and then you must deal with the real you–the good, the bad, and the ugly! To be honest, that's the place where God wants you so he can transform you into the person he called you to be. Picture yourself as a mold of clay that the master is conforming into a vessel of honor. The heat and pressure that God puts us in is designed to do its perfect work.

The Sonship

Another identity crisis that exists in the body of Christ is not recognizing our true sonship. The Bible tells us that if we are in Christ, we are a new creature; old things are passed away, and all things are new (2 Cor. 5:17). So at salvation, we have shed the old man. Now we should embrace the new. Christ also tells us that we are joint heirs with him, so my identity is sealed; I just must walk in it. When you and I fully grasp who we have been living on the inside, we can begin to have victory in every area of our lives. Satan, the enemy of our soul, will try to keep your true self hidden from you to keep you in bondage. As I look back on the last twenty-five years of my Christian walk, many of the years were lived by a man who really did not understand who he was in Christ. I read the stories in the Bible, and I sat through countless sermons, but only when the Holy Ghost taught me about my sonship in the Spirit was I able to truly live free.

Many saints are living, but finding true peace and freedom alludes them. The church is full of saints who are oppressed by their circumstances. If only they could realize the power they possess in Christ to be liberated! If we stop and remember Jacob in the Bible, he lived as a heathen for many years: Jacob lied and manipulated to get his way (see the book of Genesis). In fact, his name means "supplanter" or "cheater" (Gen. 27:36)! Jacob was having an identity crisis, and only after God got a hold of his character was his name changed from Jacob to Israel (Gen. 32:22–32). As a believer, when we live outside of the confines of God's word, we are living beneath our privilege. Now I'm going to make a very silly statement to illustrate my point. Picture you and your family at your local zoo, and you decide to visit your favorite exhibit. Let's say, the monkey cages are your favorite. Once you observe the monkeys, you enter their cage and start eating their dung! This is obviously very gross and beneath you as a human being. This is what we do when we sin against the Most High God. Only when we hate the sight and despise sin to the core can we get true deliverance. We can begin to see God transform our lives into something that pleases him. Before I gave my life to Christ, I enjoyed the sin of fornication with many women. For years after I gave my life to God, I would give my testimony about my pre-Christ addiction to the opposite sex with pride because somewhere deep inside, I was still proud of how many notches I had on my belt. Only when I realized that my sin was a true violation of God's law and that it broke the heart of the Savior who died for me did I stop feeling that pride.

The Achievement Trap

Another major obstacle of recognizing your true identity is the achievement trap. This is when you find your validation or worth in something you can achieve. Many people find this in their careers, their social circles, how much money they have in the bank, and even in the church. Although any of these can be great accomplishments, you should never find your worth or identity in anything but Christ. My wife is the love of my life, and I consider our marriage of twenty years a great achievement; but it would be foolish of me to build my life around only her. My identity is not found in my great love for her nor in our lasting marriage but only in Christ. God has called me to preach the gospel, and the fact that I'm writing this book is a testament to the redemptive work of Jesus. However, even though he called me to work for him in this capacity, my validation is not found in achieving this work. Only when I recognize that I'm complete in him will I not fall prey to trying to obtain validation from anything else in my life. Everything I accomplish for the remainder of my life is the by-product of my relationship with him.

The real danger of finding your worth in something external is that when you fail—and believe me, you will fail—you can end up becoming very discouraged because the thing you put your trust in did not manifest the way you planned. If I could be honest for a moment, I have failed more than I have ever succeeded, but in my weakness and failures, God has taught me about his love and grace. If we can begin to accept that failure is a way of life and embrace our failures as learning opportunities, we can realize that everything does work together for our good (8:28). I love sports because sports can give a real picture of life's ups and downs. Imagine a baseball player who hits an average of three out of ten every time he is at the plate. This is a weakly 30 percent average, but in baseball, this guy is a major force to be reckoned with. This player fails 70 percent of the time, but the emphasis is on continuing to persevere, knowing ultimately that success will come. The evolution of the Christ-centered life is going to shape your identity to be who God has called you to be. Our focus should be on bringing God pleasure, and everything else is secondary to this fact. My identity in Christ is not based on anything I do.

He loves me no matter what the circumstances reflect, and I can rest in this fact. Knowing that my worth is not based on my accomplishments pulls all striving and my human efforts out of the equation.

Never Settle for Less

Once you get a true definition of your identity in Christ, it's important that you never settle for anything less than what he has ordained for you. Many of us never reach our full potential due to fear. We just flounder instead of soaring with the eagles. As Christians, we are victorious by the blood of Jesus! If something is keeping us from walking and living in victory, we are settling. Period. Will we experience tough times? Yes, we will, but we should never just live to only exist. Let's look at the life of Gideon in Judges, chapter 6. Gideon is what we call today a Chicken Little. I call him a Chicken Little because of his lack of faith initially, but Gideon was called a mighty man of valor by God before he had even embarked on the mission God had for him. What's important for us to realize is that God was not limited by Gideon's limitations, and God's will was fulfilled once Gideon believed what God had declared about him. We must understand that God has a purpose for each of us to accomplish, and I believe when we stand before God, he will hold us accountable. As you continue to grow in developing a Christ-centered life, your new identity in Christ must begin to rise to the forefront of your life. Every chain and bondage that's held you captive must be cut away by the Holy Ghost so that you can walk in the newness of life. This transformation is not for the faint of heart; this is for the person who wants God more than life itself. In Jeremiah 29:13, Gods says, "Ye shall seek me, and find me, when ye shall search for me with all your heart." The transformation into our new identity starts and finishes with Christ. I'm to live here on earth physically, and I'm to rule and reign simultaneously in the spiritual realm. The truth of my existence is: I'm a spiritual being first, and the physical part of my self is secondary.

Now that I know that I'm a spiritual being first, I can begin to gravitate toward God's plan in my life. Because many of us in the body of Christ have no real concept of who we are, we spend years trying to fit into a label that many times doesn't fit. It's almost like a fish who is designed to swim trying to fly like a bird only to realize that the fish has gills and not wings. Many of us try to function out of place just to get the validation of others. Only when you recognize that you have a unique God-given purpose can you rise and make a real contribution to this planet. My God-given purpose is not limited by my upbringing or anything on this earth; my purpose was declared and prepared for me before the foundations of the world. I believe that God has placed greatness in every one of us, and we must take this journey of discovery to become everything that God wants us to be. The real challenge is getting out of our human logic and embracing the word of God, walking it out in full assurance of what God has spoken over us.

Another obstacle that hinders many believers is that we don't want to put the work in. If you are going to be great for Christ, you must commit to a life of growth. Just like an Olympic athlete, you must prepare constantly for the competition of life. Now keep in mind we already have the victory in Jesus, but we must learn to follow the direction of the Holy Ghost. As a man or woman of God, if Satan can keep you in the dark about your identity, he can keep you from walking in your God-given authority. The evolution of a Christ-centered life hinges on your recognizing of your new authority in Christ and changing your mind and heart to line up with this new identity. It's equivalent to changing your computer operating system. Once you make this change in a computer, the old system becomes obsolete. The same thing is true of embracing a new spiritual operating system according to God's holy word.

The evolution can only take place when the spirit is the driving force in your life. Your new identity is wrapped up and consumed by learning and adapting to the direction that the Holy Ghost provides. Only then can you truly live a Christ-centered life.

CHAPTER 6

Personal Inventory and Spiritual Discipline

*Let all bitterness, and wrath, and anger, and clamour, and evil
speaking, be put away with you, with all malice.*

–Ephesians 4:31 KJV

PERSONAL INVENTORY OF our lives and spiritual discipline are very important in growing in the things of God. Unfortunately, many Christians are not honest about their lives and personal struggles. Somehow, we have adopted this mentality that we have to appear as though we have everything together, and the truth of the matter is that God sees every weakness we possess and desires to set us free. I'm amazed at altar calls when a preacher proclaims God's word, offers deliverance, and someone who is in bondage would rather remain in a life of chains instead of going up to the altar and being set free. Picture someone who has a natural illness. We know that the local hospital has a free cure, but the individual who is sick decided to remain outside of the hospital. We would be shaking our head with disbelief, but many saints and sinners alike hear the word and choose to take no action. Until you begin to allow God to show you the inventory of your heart, you will continue to walk a mediocre Christian walk. When I got to this part in my Christian life, I admit it was very painful. I began to notice the sins that consumed the hidden areas of my soul.

Inventory of the Heart

Some sins are obvious, and we quickly take an inventory and try our best not to commit these acts. Sins like lying and adultery are sins committed in the open, so we put a lot of emphasis on breaking free from these. Sins like envy, strife, and malice are sins that sit in the corridors of our hearts. These sins get little attention until you are trying to go into the deeper depths of Christ. As humans we try to categorize sin as small and big, but in the eyes of God, all sin is evil and stinks in his nostrils. So when you decide to live a truly Christ-centered life, God is going to take inventory so he can begin to clean house. For years I justified my anger and jealousy only to realize that if I wanted to be used mightily by God, sin had no place in my life. We must realize that the closer we get to the light of God, the more the imperfections in our lives are exposed. He literally wants to conform us to the image of perfection. The perfection that God desires in our lives can only come to pass by the power of Jesus. I'm not talking about willpower or anything that's masked in humanity, but true conviction is surrendering to the purposes of God.

True conviction for the saint should be viewed as a good thing because God is cutting away the old and replacing it with the new. The evolution of a Christ-centered life can only take place when the inventory of our sin has been exposed so we can repent. Inventory is a daily process that will have you seeking the Father for repentance, which leads to growth and fruitfulness. I now understand that if something is in my life and it's not bringing forth godly fruit, I must assess and take inventory, then allow God to remove it. I want to make sure that we understand we are not doing an inventory to be saved because our salvation is by grace and not by works. This is the willful surrender to God's pruning process.

Spiritual Discipline

Spiritual discipline goes hand and hand with God's pruning process because it's the art of growing beyond the desires of the flesh and learning godly disciplines. As Christians, we should strive to be disciples of Christ. Again, I must emphasize that works are not the foundation for salvation, but our spiritual discipline helps us to be productive for the kingdom of God. Our military trains constantly to be prepared for the real battle, and our spiritual discipline prepares us for war with the enemy of our souls. In prayer I learn to hear from God, so if I'm ever in a life and death situation, I will be familiar with the voice of God. However, if I never utilize the discipline of prayer, I will not be familiar with the voice of God. The cost could be deadly! To be honest, I really had an internal debate within myself about adding the principle of spiritual discipline because I don't want anyone to misinterpret me saying that our works build any validity in our Christian walk. The disciplines are to be performed because I am in love with Jesus and I want to honor him in my daily life. Spiritual discipline does not make God love me more; his love for me is the same no matter how I perform. I read the Bible, pray, fast, and preach because of a desire in my heart to see others saved. I also began to experience more of his presence by spending time with my Savior. A great athlete trains the body to be an instrument for whatever sport he or she is trying to master, and if our approach is to learn and be proficient in the things of the spirit, we must live a life of spiritual preparation.

Paul told his followers to study the Word (2 Tim. 2:15). The context of this statement implies a life of discipline and constant learning. As we learn to walk and abide in the word of God, our lives will begin to mirror and emulate the life of Jesus. The Bible is full of examples of mentor-mentee relationship that shows the act of learning and training under someone who is more mature. I believe God constantly works through impartation. I have a spiritual father in the faith, and I'm often told that I sound and preach just like him. Obviously because I sat under his teaching for almost ten years, I gleaned some of his disciplines and mannerisms. Paul was the spiritual father to Timothy, and Joshua followed Moses for years before he was ready to lead Israel into the promise land. The disciples followed Jesus for a period of three years where they learned the principles of the kingdom. Discipline at its core is not bad unless you rely on it for your righteousness. We only embrace discipline in an effort to grow in the things of God so that we can be an effective witness.

The Christ-centered life consists of a person who has transformed his or her life to reflect the image of Christ. This life is a daily decision that requires you to press beyond the comforts of normal Christianity, and it propels you to a place of constant discipline and inventory. As I look into the mirror of God's word, I see a true reflection of where I'm at in my spiritual walk. In the natural, if I take a look at my reflection in a mirror, it's going to reflect my image for what it is, not what I want it to be. Only when I make changes to my hair or clothing does the image change, and the same thing applies to our spiritual walk. As we gaze into the light of the Holy Bible, we can begin to allow God's word to change us to his image.

In closing, our walk as Christians consists of a constant evolution. If we surrender, we will honor our Savior and bring forth much fruit. As a fruit gardener, our Heavenly Father will constantly prune and cut back our lives to bring forth much fruit (see John, chapter 15). God requires inventory to ensure that we are fruitful for his kingdom. Only when we are sincere about the changes that God wants to make can we really enjoy the true benefits of being a Christ-centered Christian. Beginning in chapter 2 of the book of Revelations, God is speaking to the angels or leaders of the various churches. He is essentially taking inventory and asking the churches to make the appropriate changes in order to be productive and bring him glory. So today, embrace the prompting of the Holy Spirit to allow God to extract ungodly habits and traits, and we will truly see the Glory of God revealed in our lives.

CHAPTER 7

Learning to Suffer

If we suffer, we shall also reign with him.

–2 Timothy 2:12 KJV

A S WE CONTINUE our quest into an evolution of a Christ-centered life, we must understand the principle of suffering. Paul stated in 2 Timothy 2:12, "If we suffer, we shall also reign with him." If we want to reign and see his glory, we must be prepared to suffer for our Savior. Jesus told us that we should count the cost (Luke 14:27–28). In other words, we need to understand that if we really want to grow in God, it requires us to be ready to suffer. Apostle Paul's writings have a major theme of suffering and turmoil. In fact, at the point of Paul's conversion, the Holy Ghost told Ananias that Paul was a chosen vessel (which sounds good), but if you dig further, God tells Ananias that Paul was chosen to suffer for the sake of the gospel (Acts 9:15–16). Now as I read this depiction of this story, I'm amazed at the context of the conversation. God didn't say that Paul would establish churches. God didn't say Paul would write the majority of the New Testament. God put the emphasis on the suffering that Paul would have to endure for the gospel. We as believers in the twenty-first century can't escape this mandate if we truly want to know the God of the Bible. When we understand that the gospel involves suffering, we can then trust God through the trials of life. I admit when I first gave my life to God, I felt that it was God's responsibility to make sure I never suffered and that my life was smooth and trial-free. But God's methods of getting the glory is contrary to a life of comfort at all points. God does want us to enjoy life, and he still works many miracles to show that he is faithful, but I must realize that it rains on the just as well as the unjust. The difference is that he is with me in my storms.

A Great Cloud of Witnesses

The Bible is full of believers who our God allowed to suffer for his purpose and plan. Once we understand that trials are a natural part of being a Christian, we won't get bent out of shape when we are in the midst of a storm. Learning to endure our test comes with maturity, and it gives us a new awareness of faith. My sufferings, which are only temporary on this earth, draw me closer to my God, and they teach me how to trust God in any situation. The Bible teaches us that we are predestined to be sons and daughters of God (Eph. 1:5). When we grasp the truth of predestination, we will begin to understand that God, the One who created heaven and earth, is sovereign and in control.

Most modern Christians are content to have a mediocre relationship with God until they are in need. When we are in turmoil, our prayer life changes, our spiritual focus is sharper, and we pursue God with more hunger and passion. This book was birthed out of my own pain and sorrow. I would love to say that I woke up saved, and every day I pursued God like Paul or King David, but the truth is that my Christ-centered evolution only came when I found myself in deep water. I cried out to God with all my heart, and he was there to rescue me out of the abyss. As discussed earlier, Paul had themes of suffering and learning to be content throughout his writings. We see one instance where he prayed to God to alleviate the pressure, and God told him *no* and that his grace is sufficient (2 Cor. 12:9).

Hold up. Stop.

Are you telling me that God wanted him to continue to suffer, and that he was going to have to trust God in the middle of his test? *Exactly.* This is the truth of the gospel. We are in a battle, and sometimes, we are going to get hurt and injured. The good news is that if you are in Christ, he has already overcome the world, so you don't have to be a prisoner to the power of the trial. Your suffering may never feel good, but as you learn to rest and trust in our Savior, you will begin to get a new appreciation for what you are going through. Paul teaches us that when we are weak, then we are strong because we no longer depend on human power and ability (2 Cor. 12:10). Now we can activate a power on the inside of ourselves. I've been guilty of preaching victory after victory: the splitting of the Red Sea, David killing the Giant, Joshua crossing the Jordan, and many more. Now don't get me wrong. I believe that in Christ, we are victorious, but we must preach the necessity of suffering and the benefits that our Heavenly Father has designed it for.

The Fellowship of His Suffering

One of the most important disciplines we will ever encounter is the fellowship of Christ's suffering. Learning to suffer for Christ builds intimacy and helps increase our faith in the power of God. The suffering that we face on this earth cannot be compared to the glory that God will reveal to us in eternity (Rom. 8:18). Paul teaches us to become a person who is content in any situation because ultimately, God controls everything, and God's plans are perfect. The question must be asked: how much intimacy do you really want from God? I ask this because if you want true fellowship and communion, the vehicle God uses many times is our sufferings. My sufferings propel me into a place of seeking and taking refuge in his presence. Once I'm in his presence, I gain a new level of communion, and my fellowship is taken to a new level. My pastor would always tell me that God is more concerned about our personal character above everything else. Every teardrop, every sleepless night drove me to a place of crying out to my Savior, and he revealed himself to me in a new and fresh way.

David is called a man after God's heart, but if you read throughout the book of Psalms, much of his life was full of trouble. Some of his issues were self-inflicted, and some were just trials God allowed, but David learned to run to God for his every need. If you want to live a Christ-centered life, you must allow the trial to accomplish its purpose in your life. Christ took on the ultimate suffering on the cross for our sins, and we can rest in the fact that we have the victory because of his redemptive work on the cross. The cross has become a symbol that many Christians wear around their necks for a fashion statement, but when we understand what Jesus endured for mankind and that the cross represents suffering, we will never approach the cross the same. Jesus tells us to pick up our cross daily (Luke 9:23), or in other words, be prepared to suffer daily for the cause of Christ. In Romans 8:36, the writer tells us that as believers, we are accounted as sheep headed for the slaughter. My very existence should be to lay this life down for the glory of God to be revealed. If you are to rise to a level of a true disciple of Jesus, you must be prepared daily to suffer, and in your sufferings, you will experience the fellowship you have been longing for.

Obedience and Suffering

The Bible tells us plainly that Jesus learned obedience through the things he suffered. Keep in mind that Jesus was sinless; he never violated the commandments nor the precepts of God, but he was ordained to suffer for the glory of the Heavenly Father. The object lesson is that all believers will have their fair share of suffering. If we recognize that it's a part of our lives, we can then seek what God is attempting to reveal to us in these moments in our lives. We are not perfect like Christ, but we have been made perfect; and we are now in right standing with God because of Jesus. So we must become obedient even to the point of major suffering. When it comes to pain, many Christians run for the hills. We try to avoid tough times at all cost, but God teaches us in the scripture that we should count it all joy when we encounter trials and tribulations (Jas 1:2–3). When we are in the midst of our suffering, God is revealing to us what's in the inside of our hearts. Let's compare the suffering process to the process of extracting olive oil. The olive oil extraction process is quite a phenomenon. The oil is only released once the olives have been crushed and put under tremendous stress. At this point in the process, the person is able to get the valuable oil, and the same holds true in the life of a Christian. Our God will allow us to suffer and become crushed so he can get the most valuable part of us out into the world. If you could have an honest conversation with many of the people we admire, whether they are in the church or not, you will notice a common theme of perseverance through tough times that allowed them to finally reach a place of success. The Bible tells us, "Many are the afflictions of the righteous, but the LORD delivereth him out of them all" (Ps. 34:19). God is telling us in this popular psalm that we as Christians will face many trials and tribulations, but we can rest assure that our God is a deliverer. We can truly trust him in the midst of life's storms.

So as we begin the process of changing our thinking, we should look for God's hand in the middle of our sufferings. Only when we reach this point in our spiritual walk can we echo the words of Paul: "For I reckoned that the sufferings of this present time are not worthy to be compared with the glory which shall be revealed in us" (Rom. 8:18). As believers in Jesus, we must recognize that we are on this earth for a time, but our future abode is with the King of kings in heaven. Once this truth comes alive in your heart, you can begin to see tough times as a test that God has ordained. Then you'll be able to keep your spiritual composure in hard times. The truth of the matter is that many of us lose our spiritual bearings, and we find ourselves out of the will of God because of the trials we may be facing. I wish I could say I never went berserk in the middle of a test, but I was quite the opposite. I was very emotional and would fly off in an emotional tirade. Sometimes it took me months to find my way back to the will of God, but the great news of our Savior is that he is truly a God of forgiveness.

I remember one incident that happened early on in my ministry. My cousin asked me to marry him and his new wife, and I was honored to take on the task. I practiced the ceremony for months. I had my lines down, and I was ready for everyone to take me seriously as a minister of the gospel. The big day came, and I was dressed in my collar and ready to prove to the world that I was really called by the Lord. The wedding started off great. The bridesmaids and groomsmen came in the room, and everyone applauded. The bride came to the altar on cue, and now it was time for me to recite my lines as I had rehearsed for months. I remember getting to the point in the ceremony when I asked for the rings, and my next memory was getting an IV in an ambulance. I fainted; I collapsed in the middle of the ceremony! I was so embarrassed! I told God I never wanted to stand in front of people again. I cried. I honestly did not attend church for an entire month. How could my God allow me to get ridiculed to this level? I thought he loved me! I felt like a failure, and I didn't want to go on. But what I learned through this pain and suffering is that God's grace is sufficient. He took one of the worst experiences in my life and taught me humility and how to depend on him for everything. Suffering that drives you to Christ is truly a blessing, and the dividends are huge. Learn to suffer for Christ and you will get a closer walk with the Father. That's the real goal of a Christ-centered life.

CHAPTER 8

Walking by Faith

For we walk by faith, not by sight.

–2 Corinthians 5:7 KJV

A CHRIST-CENTERED LIFE is a life of faith. As you begin to grow in this evolution, you must become a man or woman of faith. The very foundation of Christianity is based on faith. We must believe that God exists by faith and that he is a rewarder of those who seek him out (Heb. 11:6). As a man or woman of God, you must learn to walk by faith. Most believers struggle with this concept because it goes contrary to the five natural senses. Only when you embrace faith as a way of life can you enjoy the deep things of the gospel. The Bible teaches us that if we do not have faith, we cannot please God (Heb. 11:6), so in order to please and honor our Heavenly Father, we must make faith a natural reflex in our lives. When you think of the word reflex, you think of the word automatic. So when we are facing situations in our lives, we must see them automatically through the eyes of faith, and then we can transform this world for Jesus. Now the question must be asked: what is faith? Hebrews 11:1 says that faith is the substance of things hoped for, the evidence of things not seen. Our faith is built on the substance of what we know, not on what our natural eyes perceive.

Jesus told his disciple Thomas, "Blessed are they that have not seen, and yet have believed" (John 20:29). God wants us to trust him beyond our circumstances. That only comes by a mature faith that developed in the fire. I trust my wife completely because she has shown herself to be trustworthy through a twenty-year relationship. The same thing holds true to my Heavenly Father: he has demonstrated his faithfulness over and over again. The Bible says we go from faith to faith (Rom. 1:17), so that implies different levels of faith that God takes us through. Faith at its core is trusting God. Real faith requires us to live with the question: are we willing to trust God when we don't have all the answers? If you can grasp within your heart that God moves in mysterious ways, you can understand the dynamics of faith. I wish God gave us a detailed map of every move because it would make life a lot easier. The truth of our God is that he enjoys the concept of a person depending totally on him, one who is walking and moving by faith. Think about it. If you had all the answers, you wouldn't need faith, but because God only is pleased by faith, he only gives you what you need to continue to trust him. If you read Hebrews 11, you can see a chronicle of exploits that believers accomplished, and the common theme is faith in our God. The miracles and exploits were performed because someone dared to have faith in the God of the Bible. Our evidence is found in the word of God. The Bible says that faith comes by hearing, and hearing by the word of God (Rom. 10:17). So if I'm to walk and live in faith, it must be grounded in God's holy scripture.

Shield of Faith

In the book of Ephesians, Paul is outlining the whole armor of God. He makes a key statement when he says, "Above all, taking the shield of faith, wherewith ye shall be able to quench all the fiery darts of the wicked" (Eph. 6:16). Paul is telling us that our faith will enable us to combat the attacks of the evil one if we learn to embrace what God has declared in our lives. The shield in battle is designed to block or inhibit the attacks of an enemy. The shield is primarily a defensive weapon, but if utilized properly, it can save one's life when in battle. The shield is designed to block the arrows, or accusations, that Satan tosses at us. It allows protection for the vital parts of our lives not to be touched by the devil. Faith is trusting in God's word to move you beyond the natural circumstances you are facing. The devil magnifies our problems to keep us discouraged and depressed, but with the shield of faith, you prohibit the darts of doubt from infiltrating your mind and heart. As a child, one of my favorite superheroes was Captain America. His primary weapon was his shield, and he would use it to deflect the offensive attacks of his enemies. As a Christian, the shield of faith will help us maintain a godly balance and make this evolution a true reality.

As long as we live on this earth, our adversary will always try to destroy our lives with tactics that attempt to push us out of the arena of faith and confront our troubles in the flesh. This will ultimately be deadly in the lives of Christians. The devil is on a constant mission to have us resort to dealing with our problems with the arm of the flesh. We need to understand that flesh begets flesh, and we can never get the spiritual victories we desire by following the leading of the flesh. Faith taps into the power of the spirit, and it transforms our very core into a person who really lives by faith. The evolution of a Christ-centered life will never be recognized without living by faith. Every person in the Bible used majorly by God became a person of faith, and God used them to accomplish major exploits. If you want the things of the spirit, you have to weave faith into your spiritual DNA.

Faith goes beyond simple belief. Real faith will show up in your actions. When you truly trust and have faith in God, your movements will be in sync with your belief system. My hope is that as you continue to read this book, your belief system transforms to line up with the will of God for your life. When I say belief system, I'm talking about what you believe to the core of who you are. When God has changed you to the core, everything changes; and you are ready to experience a new level of faith. The type of faith that makes the devil nervous when you show up the scene. True faith can transform everything in your life, but another aspect of faith is that it gives you the ability to endure any trial or tribulation that you may face. Real faith is the mark of a Christian who has allowed the evolution of a Christ-centered existence to be dominant in his or her life. Apostle Paul, Apostle Peter, and numerous biblical Christians were able to endure all manner of pain because of one reason: *faith* in our God. As you continue this journey of discovering your place in God's plan, faith will be paramount to everything in your spiritual life.

CHAPTER 9

A Matter of Character

A Good name is more desirable than great riches; to be esteemed is better than silver or Gold.

–Proverbs 22:1 (a) KJV

THE FINAL CHAPTER of the evolution of a Christ-centered life is the aspect of character. Godly character is the true mark of Jesus being Lord of your life. Character is learning to do the right thing when no one else is around. Many Christians learn to behave properly around people they respect and want to make a good impression on, but God sees everything; and once we commit to displaying true character in every facet of our lives, true spiritual fruit will be manifested. Joyce Meyers, one of my favorite teachers, gives an awesome example of this in one of her teachings. She talks about how God would convict her about putting the shopping cart back in the proper location. I believe once you become accustomed to the smaller character victories, the large ones will be automatic. I realize that as you read this book, it may seem very difficult to raise your moral compass, but as a believer, our true example is Jesus. Will I fall? Of course, I will! But when godly character is formed by the Holy Ghost, you can experience days of victory after victory. Character starts within our hearts, and only God can make a change in our lives. Human beings, by nature, are depraved, and once we understand our need for a savior, Jesus will spend a lifetime developing our character. Most Christians are aware of the big issues such as stealing, killing, etc., but God is concerned about every character defect, from the so-called white lie to the occasional glimpse at the opposite sex. Godly character may be the toughest lesson you will ever face, but the rewards are truly eternal. I believe that godly character propels you into the true riches in Christ, and it allows God to move and act on your behalf. As believers, the devil wants us to compromise on the precepts and commandments of God because he understands that in many instances, this disqualifies us from the protection and promises of God. Character will sometimes allude us, and it takes some real spiritual fortitude to press on through. The culture of the world, and sometimes the church, sets us up to compromise the God of the Bible, but ultimately, it leads to destruction. We must understand that our character should glorify our Heavenly Father. In Matthew 5:16, the Bible tells us to let our lights so shine before men that they may see our good works and glorify our Father who is in heaven. God's desire for us is that we learn to be a person of high integrity and character. Once people recognize this evidence in our lives, it points them to God who is the source of our transformed character. The biggest indicator that shows your growth in the spirit is the fact that God has made a sincere change in your spirit man. Many people who lack character, even though they are anointed and have extensive talent, always seem to fall from grace because talent can elevate you, but character will keep you in the place of promise.

As we said earlier, most of us have heard the horror stories of someone we have held in high esteem only to read or hear about them being involved in activities that are so outside of who you thought they were. Character is the Holy Spirit prompting you to do the will of God, and it's not going to be always easy because of the flesh. The true test of character may force you to suffer in the flesh, but if you grasp true character, the rewards are eternal. The evolution of a Christ-centered life is learning how to allow the glory on the inside manifest to the outside, and this will show up in your life as a person with high values and character. It's not just simply doing the right thing, but it becomes a lifestyle change that gives a fresh aroma in every area of your Christian walk.

Character Has to Be Intentional

The practice of godly character has to be intentional. If you believe that you can find yourself in a compromising situation and your flesh is going to allow you the chance to make the correct choice, you have sincerely underestimated the draw of your own flesh. I have come to realize that I don't trust my flesh in any circumstance. So the way I get constant victory is that I constantly practice godly decisions intentionally. For example, no matter how innocent it may be, I will never have lunch with another female alone, besides my wife, because I don't trust the flesh or the circumstance. Godly character is comprised of intentional godly decisions that will never force you to be in any circumstance that tempts you to compromise your integrity. The majority of people who end up in major situations started out in smaller ones that eventually snowballed into a horrific ordeal that may have been avoided if they weren't in a compromising position. David, before he ever had an adulterous affair with Bathsheba, was in the wrong place at the wrong time, and it led to him violating the laws of God. Using the analogy of a snowball on a hill, it can start out as the size of a pebble. And if it continues to gain momentum, it will eventually be a major boulder that no one can move. Imagine if you become so disciplined that the pebble is not placed on the hill, and you never run the risk of anything becoming a boulder. That's how you get the victories in your life. Joseph as a servant in Potiphar's house was such a man of high character that when he was approached by his master's wife, he had the spiritual fortitude to reject her advances. The honor and character started way before he was tempted. He made a life decision to never dishonor his God. If you think you can be engulfed in some sort of sin and you will make the right decision, you are very naive, and you are setting yourself up for failure. The way to always get the victory is to never align with the forbidden act. Character cuts the behavior off at its root and thrives on following God's holy commandments. I want to drive the point home that we are not saved by our works, but our works show a transformation by the spirit in our lives. True character is a way of life, and if you can allow God to do this work in your life, the evolution will transform your life.

Character, in my opinion, will be the biggest indicator that the Christ-centered life is really taking place in your heart. Character is an inward conviction that manifest to the outside. It's the power source that molds your decisions and propels you to a life of godly behavior. I'm not talking about human efforts of bending your will to follow some human moral code only to fall because your will power has finally collapse, but when the Holy Ghost is the driving force behind the character change, the fruit is consistent for the remainder of your life. One of the ways I knew God was really doing a major work in my life is when I begin to share my personal testimony with people, and they could not believe that I was involved in some of the area I was describing to them. Jacob, prior to God's changing his name to Israel, was a deceiver and liar. Once he wrestled with God, he was miraculously transformed from Jacob the Supplanter to Israel, which means God-contended.

Our Savior specializes in invading our wills to ensure that we become men and women with high godly character.

Refining Character

The concept of refining is not a new concept, but it is the process that God uses to conform our character. When you understand the true refinery process, you will realize that it's designed to burn out all the impurities in our lives. The fire refines and purifies us to accomplish the will of our Heavenly Father. When you have gold or silver and it's exposed to high levels of heat, it separates the impurities and completely burns them out–the same holds true in our lives. When God turns up the heat in our lives, he is trying to burn away the impurities in our character. This process can leave a man or woman feeling abandoned and forsaken by God, but when you recognize that he is conforming you to the image of our savior Jesus, you will learn to embrace the process. The refining fire of the Holy Ghost is designed to burn, but not consume; it's the power that God invades our lives to cut away the sin that easily ensnares us. The majority of Christians in the modern church fight this process with everything in their being. We have become a church of people pleasers instead of a people of change. We design social programs to fit into our lives instead of fitting our lives into the pattern of the Holy Ghost. Only when I abandon myself for the cause of Christ will I see the evolution begin to manifest. Character is the one thing you cannot fake because whatever is in you will eventually rise to the surface. The refining process is designed to bring the matter to the surface in order to get rid of the impurities in our lives. Refining one's character is a lifelong quest. There were issues I dealt with when I first got saved that God immediately delivered me from, and there are some issues that still plague me to this very day. I believe that as I continue to, Christ will spend a lifetime of perfecting certain areas in my life. King David, at the end of his life, had several virgins lying in his bed to give him heat, and the Bible says that he didn't touch one sexually, but David in his younger years got tempted with the very appearance of Bathsheba. Character is. If we take heed to the leading of the spirit, we will always find ourselves growing in this area.

Refining is always a mark of God building maturity in your life, and it's the tag of a future of continual obedience in your life. We learn obedience many times from the things we suffer. God will many times use trials to refine and teach us obedience to walk in a level of greater character. I remember at the age of nineteen when I enlisted in the US Army. I went to basic training with a street mentality, and I was like any other red-blooded American boy–very selfish and was only concerned about myself. The Army Basic Training is designed to take a rough-around-the-edges person and produce a soldier fit to be utilized by the US Army. They designed their training to remove individuality and have a group of people from all different backgrounds to operate as one. This process, if you can imagine, is tedious and grueling, but the end results speak for themselves. Our lives as Christians are such that if we allow the Refiner who is God to really cut away at our character, the sky is the limit. God's desire is that we shine on the earth like pure gold, and for gold to really come forth, it takes being in the fire to produce the best results. My character will only produce godly results after spending time in the fire.

The evolution of a Christ-centered life will show itself true once my character has been refined. The quest to drawing closer to God and really making a difference on earth can only take place once we commit to honoring God in our lives. If you have Christians who are committed to prayer, fasting, and a life of true character, the devil knows this is a lethal combination to the kingdom of darkness. I'm not, by any means, saying that it requires us to be perfect, but someone who is striving each and every day to bring glory to God will make an impact on this earth. Ask yourself this question: do you want to be a world-changer for Christ? If the answer is yes, start by walking and living in a place of godly character. Character is the one thing that cannot be duplicated. If you remember in the Bible when Moses threw down his staff, the evil sorcerers of Pharaoh were able to duplicate the first couple of miracles. The anti-Christ in the last days will be able to perform miracles, but godly character can only be produced by the Holy Spirit in the life of a believer who is committed to honoring Jesus in their everyday life. The church does not have a shortage of gifts and talents, and we are full of people who can teach and preach the word of God. But if we are to take a real honest assessment, we are seriously lacking in the area of true God-honoring character. The devil knows that as long as he has a foothold in the character of the body of Christ, he can limit our impact on the earth. The evolution of our spiritual lives has to include God refining our character. As you grasp the material in this book, the one point that ties every chapter together is godly character. I believe, once you put everything in this book in place in your life, your character will begin to reflect the essence of our savior Jesus. The church in the last days will be responsible for taking the gospel to the ends of the earth. Without character that reflects Christ, this task will not happen. If I can be transparent for a moment, my biggest struggle in my personal walk was my issues with character. I could pray and read the Bible for hours, but until I learned how to put what I was reading and praying about into practice, I could only see minor results.

I'm going to make a very controversial statement that I know is true: the fact that someone is a Christian doesn't guarantee that they possess high character. Unfortunately, in my years of walking with Christ, I have met individuals who I believed were true believers but really struggled in the area of godly character. One thing you can rest assured is that Jesus will spend your entire life conforming you to the image of Christ. Our character will be tested until the day we die, and we must realize that the mark of a true disciple of Christ is the mark of high character. My character defines who I am at the core of my being, beyond the church steeple, beyond impressing the pastor. My character is the very thing that makes me tick, it's the conviction of who I am when no one else is around. It's the one that will eventually stand before God on judgment day. When I comprehend that God sees everything that happens in my life and there is nothing hidden that will not be revealed, I will understand the gravity of living every moment to please him in every way. True character is only interested in living the truth no matter how it feels to the flesh. The Bible is full of individuals who lived a life of godly character, and it is also filled with people who decided to walk a life of sin. And if we pay close attention to their stories, we can get a real picture of the benefits of learning to yield to the Holy Spirit in the area of godly character. My prayer and desire is that as you come to the end of this book, you take a real close look at your walk with Jesus and that you learn to allow the evolution of a Christ-centered life to become a personal mandate. My hope for you is that this triggers a life full of glory and hunger for our Savior who came to save the whole world.

CONCLUSION

IN CONCLUSION, THE evolution of a Christ-centered life will change the type of Christian you become. Only when you allow the God of the universe to transform who you are at the core will you experience the power of a true relationship with Christ. Sometimes we make unrealistic expectations when we read a book or hear a sermon, and we look for immediate or superfast results. If I can be completely honest, this transformation may take years, but I guarantee that the journey, though it may be long, will be well worth your time. In fact, the results will be eternal. That's the great news about the gospel: if we are in Christ Jesus, we are truly eternal beings.

ABOUT THE AUTHOR

CALVIN BARNES JR. has been a minister of the gospel of Jesus Christ for a period of twenty-three years. He accepted his call to ministry in August 1997. Mr. Barnes also served as an elder for Word Alive Christian Church for a decade and has a weekly radio ministry that reaches many with the message of the cross. Calvin resides in Northwest Florida with his wife, Marsha, and their children.

INDEX

E

evolution
    constant, 41
    true, 6

F

faith (religious), 2–3, 9, 13, 30, 37, 41, 44–45, 48–50
fasting, 14–15, 55

G

Gideon, 37
God, names of
    Heavenly Father, 3, 27, 30–31, 33, 41, 45–46, 48–49, 52, 54
    Holy Ghost, 8, 12–13, 16, 26, 28–29, 35, 37–38, 43, 51, 53–54
    Holy Spirit, 6, 11, 16, 18, 24, 29, 42, 55–56
gospel (the great message of the church), 7, 13–14, 23, 36, 43–44, 47–48, 55, 57, 59
Gospels (books of the Bible), 13, 23
    John, 28
    Luke, 4, 32
    Matthew, 7, 12–13, 17, 19, 21–22, 30, 52
    See also Bible, the

H

Holy Scriptures. See Bible, the

I

identity crisis, 34–35

idolatry. See idol worship
idol worship, 1–2, 4–5, 8
Isaac, 2–3
Israel (Jacob), 35, 53
Israel (nation), 4, 7–8, 16, 25, 28, 41

K

kingdom of God, 2, 11, 23, 25, 32, 40

L

Lord's Prayer, the, 30, 32

M

Moses, 19, 25, 28, 30, 55

P

prayer, 15, 27–30, 32–33, 40, 55
prayer closet, 29–30

S

salvation, 8, 28, 35, 40
Satan, 16–17, 35, 38. See also devil
Solomon (king), 5
spiritual discipline, 40–41

T

temptation, 17–18, 31
trials, 23, 44–46, 50, 54
tribulations. See trials

W

wolves, 14–15

Lightning Source UK Ltd.
Milton Keynes UK
UKHW010706240520
363742UK00004B/120/J